HOME TRUTHS

Also by Gerald Duff

Novels

Indian Giver
Graveyard Working
That's All Right, Mama: the Unauthorized Life of Elvis's Twin
Memphis Ribs
Snake Song
Coasters

Short Stories

Fire Ants

Poetry

A Ceremony of Light
Calling Collect

HOME TRUTHS

A Deep East Texas Memory

GERALD DUFF

TCU Press
Fort Worth

Library of Congress Cataloging-in-Publication Data
Duff, Gerald.
Home truths : a deep East Texas memory / Gerald Duff.
p. cm.
ISBN 978-0-87565-435-5 (pbk. : alk. paper)
1. Duff, Gerald. 2. Authors--United States--Biography. 3. Texas, East--Biography. I. Title.
PS3554.U3177A46 2011
813'.54--dc22
[B]
2010051358

TCU Press
P. O. Box 298300
Fort Worth, Texas 76129
817.257.7822
http://www.prs.tcu.edu
To order books: 800.826.8911

Designed by Bill Brammer, fusion29.com

Portions of this book have appeared in different form in *Solstice: A Literary Magazine* and *Connotation Press*, to whose editors grateful acknowledgment is made.

In memory of my mother Dorothy Jane Irwin Duff,
my father Willie Ellis Duff,
and for my sister Nancy,
and my wife Patricia, an only child from Alabama

The eyes of Texas are upon you,
All the live long day.
The eyes of Texas are upon you,
You cannot get away.

John Sinclair

Tell all the Truth but tell it slant—
Success in Circuit lies
The Truth must dazzle gradually
Or every man be blind—

Emily Dickinson

Contents

Author's Note

A home truth is a key fact, one uncomfortable to acknowledge, and the account I offer in this book of memory represents my attempt to state home truths, to face them, and to reveal as much about them as I am able. Put another way, what I attempt is to declare the impoverishment of truth and to claim the nourishment of lies.

Growing up in the state of Texas taught me the need, use, and art of the lie. This book is an examination of my learning to lie while coming up in East Texas and on the Gulf Coast, my reasons for having to deny the truths about myself, my family, and our situation in that place and time, and how my recasting and reinterpretation of fact led inevitably to my becoming a writer of fiction.

I was born into a family with deep roots in the piney woods of East Texas on my father's side and in the solid Midwest on my mother's. My father was a working man in the petro-chemical industry in the Golden Triangle of Texas, so-called, until he lost his job at the end of World War II and moved us into his home country, the logged-out, farmed-out woods of East Texas, the remnants of culture of the settlers from the Old South who came into Texas after the Civil War.

I found myself as a child transported from the Gulf Coast into an exquisitely demarcated social structure dependent upon a settled view of the world and my family's place in it. I sought refuge in books, my imagination, and a refusal to accept what the conditions of my existence in Texas told me was right, true, and just. The themes working through the first half or so of this book relate to the food we ate, the water we drank, the church we attended, and the God we prayed to for deliverance.

"The eyes of Texas," school children still learn to sing in the Lone Star State, "are upon you, and you cannot get away." Much of my story is an account of attempting to escape in whatever ways I could imagine. My book circles around the implications, the use, the benefit, and the satisfaction of spinning lies in spite of the truth. The times in which I grew up were rife with change, redefinition of relationships sexual, racial, political, and cultural, and my memoir reflects my responses to all that. It was a time of prevarication, new views of old realities, and the personal necessity to adapt. There were lies of need and lies of convenience, and my memoir takes that into account.

A cowboy song we fourth-grade students were taught to sing in a dying East Texas town states the best core home truth of my book of memory.

I'm going to leave
Old Texas now,

They've got no use
For the longhorn cow.
They've plowed and fenced
My cattle range
And the people there
Are all so strange.

CHAPTER 1

What You're Named Is What You Are

So I was doomed. I knew that as my mother told me there was no escape from my name, and I knew that words were what doomed me. They always have.

The first memory I can recall is my being lifted over a wire fence by my father while my mother watches, and being placed down on a surface covered with snow. That was in Texas, but I didn't know it at the time. I must have been well over a year old because I can remember standing in the snow and looking up at my parents on the other side of the fence, wondering why they were beaming at me. They must have told me what the white stuff on the ground was, but I don't remember that and I don't remember being much interested in where I had been placed or the white stuff I was standing in. I did realize the two of them wanted some reaction from me, but I couldn't figure out just what that was. That puzzlement as to how I ought to react to their expectations of me did in fact set a pattern and characterized the entire course of my relationship with my parents from that day forward.

They intended what they presented of the world to me to have a certain calculated and known effect, as they saw it, and they habitually stepped back to watch me gather it in. My problem was not one of having no reaction to their proffers, but of having an impure one, a reaction composed of contradictions and second guesses. I knew they wanted something from me, but I was doomed never to know just how I should behave at such times. So my habitual response was to make something up to satisfy, to act in a way calculated to advance my state, and by so doing to be left alone to my own devices. I learned to create my own truth. I learned the wonderful use of the lie and how it could serve me.

I've always been a coward physically—as far back as I can remember and all the way up to today—and soon after that snow episode on the Texas Gulf

Coast, the first event illustrating that fact occurred. It involved a board laid over a ditch full of water which I was expected to negotiate alone. I must have successfully gotten over it on the way out of our yard, because I was coming back toward the house when the trouble began. A boy named Jimmy was blocking my way over the board, and I knew I was no match for him, of course, though he was smaller than I was. I knew he would prevail, and I knew that because I feared it. By that point, I had learned that what I dreaded was likely to happen precisely because I didn't want it to happen. Jimmy would master me because I was afraid he would.

I was shirtless, and I know that because he scratched my back hard enough to draw blood as I struggled to get by him on the board over the ditch. I was weeping before the action even started, always being good at crying, and I knew I was doomed to defeat from the beginning because I saw it coming and because the boy had a better name than I did.

His name was Jimmy, a good, solid, ordinary label, and I was called Gerald, a designation I had already learned was that of a sissy and a loser. So when Jimmy went to work with his fingernails, I hardly even pushed back, but wailed instead for my mother to rescue me. She did, explaining to me later that I'd have to learn to stand up for myself and fight back against those who opposed me. There was no comfort for me in that, and I remember crying even harder then, realizing I'd never be able to take up arms and defend myself from Jimmies and Johnnies and Bobbies, permanently hampered as I was by my weak name.

What you were called was powerful and indicative of success or the lack of it, I knew, and my parents had betrayed me at birth by naming me Gerald, adding further damage by giving me the middle name of Aldine. "Why?" I remember asking my mother. "Why am I Gerald? Why can't I be Johnny?" She didn't attempt to answer me, except to say later when I declared that I would be known as Johnny henceforth, "No, you won't be Johnny. You won't be anything but what you are. You're Gerald, and that's what you're going to be called now and forever."

I had two grandfathers, unlike my own grandchildren who have five or six at last count. One was my mother's father, Grandpa Irwin, who always wore a tie and a starched shirt, and drove a car to come see me. He brought bananas when he came, a rare treat in wartime Texas. So when he invited me to go back with him from where we lived in Hardin County to spend the night in his apartment in Beaumont (he was separated from his second wife by then), I was eager to go. I wouldn't have agreed to go with my other grandfather, my father's father, who had a full beard and lived in a log house even deeper in the country than we did. He lived with a wife who was not a real grandmother to me, and he was sick and stayed in bed all the time, even in the daytime, waiting to die, though I didn't know that was going on.

Once when I was visiting him with my parents in his log house, and my cousin Willie Vee was there, too, he asked us grandchildren to give him a kiss. That would've involved crawling up in the bed where he lay and putting our lips somewhere in that tangled mass of hair on his face. Neither of us would do that, of course, Willie Vee shaking her head *no* so hard that her hair thrashed back and forth and the tears from her eyes splashed on the floor like big raindrops.

Amos Duff then reached into a pocket and drew out two nickels, offering Willie Vee and me one each to kiss him. I immediately did what I had to do to get the money, sticking my face into that mass of whiskers and rubbing my hand across my lips afterwards until my mouth hurt. When Willie Vee continued to refuse the offer, I did it again and got the other nickel, causing all the adults crowded into the room to laugh loud enough to hurt my ears. I remember looking at them in contempt and anger, wondering what was wrong with my aunts and uncles, my mother and father, and the old man lying in the bed next to the fireplace. Nothing was funny when nickels were involved.

Willie Vee remembers that event, too, but nowadays as an older woman self-christened *Virginia* for decades, she claims she was the grandchild who traded kisses for nickels in that log house full of wood smoke, a bunch of Duff family members, and an old man lying in a bed in the daytime.

"I was the only one who kissed Grandpa," she will say, and then making the lie even bigger and better, "and I said to him I wouldn't take a nickel to do it. I'd kiss my grandpa for free as many times as he wanted."

I have to admire Virginia for that, and for the other ways she's reconstructed the past and the present over the years to suit her needs. She never finished high school, for example, dropping out in her junior year to marry a tall ducktailed electrician, destined later to become an ardent George Wallace fan, so she never attended college, of course. Yet I've heard her tell people that she was a "history major" and that she still loves the subject, making this announcement with a wonderfully wistful look on her face. Like me and most of the Duffs, Virginia learned early the need and advisability of recasting reality to make it palatable. It's the only reliable way to get through the day in East Texas.

But I did once agree to leave my home with my parents from where we lived in Hardin County to spend the night with my mother's father, my civilized grandfather Irwin, the easy access to bananas in his apartment in Beaumont on my mind, and all went well until it was time to go to bed. That was when I announced that I was ready to go home now, and the story is I did it so forcefully and tearfully that Grandpa Irwin didn't waste time trying to persuade me otherwise. So he drove me back from his apartment in Beaumont all the way into the darkness of Hardin County and home.

That part of the event I don't remember, but I can still see the hall my grandfather tried to get me to walk down toward a room where I was supposed to sleep. And that hall is dark in my memory, and narrow and threatening, and I still wouldn't want to travel it.

CHAPTER 2

God's Hospital

I WAS BORN IN HOTEL DIEU IN BEAUMONT, TEXAS, IN SEPTEMBER OF 1938. Whenever I was told that fact as I grew up, the person pronouncing the word always made *dieu* rhyme with *boo*. I don't think anybody in my family realized the words were French and one of them meant God. They knew the name of the hospital was Catholic, of course, as most strange things were in that part of Texas, the area where Louisiana laps over into the Lone Star State and exerts its warping influence. But I learned to be proud of the fact that I came into the world in a hospital with such a name. It was a mark of distinction.

That I was born in a hospital at all was worth comment, in fact, and indicated merit. My sister Nancy, three years later, was born at home, a small house in Hale Station, a railroad stop in Hardin County. But I was the first child, at least the first one of my mother's children to survive birth. I was born in Jefferson County where Spindletop, the first successful oil well in Texas, was drilled, and in a hospital dramatically named Hotel Dieu, and I was a boy. The signs were right, and all was auspicious.

My mother was the third of four children, thus the baby of the family for a period of years before she was usurped by the last one of her siblings, and she never got over the shock of having been deposed. Her father and mother were Nebraskans come to Texas in connection with John Irwin's employment with the Magnolia Oil Company, and her mother died when my mother was around eleven. John soon married a woman named Belle whom all the children hated, and I was raised to view her as an interloper and a fraudulent grandmother.

I still have a photograph of my mother Dorothy at age six or so. She stands on the front porch of a house somewhere in Nebraska, dressed all in white and bent over a toy crib filled with dolls. She looks up wistfully into the closing lens focused on her, as if she can see the long spiral down the social ladder to come: the move to Texas, the new baby sister of the family assuming her rightful role, the death of her mother, Belle installed in her mother's place, all that grief waiting to descend upon her.

Dorothy Irwin was never taller than four feet, eleven inches, but she had played basketball guard for Beaumont High on the same team with Babe Didrikson, and in her forties, sick already with the cancer that would kill her at fifty-two, could still throw a basketball the length of the court. She did that once when we happened to be walking through a gym together, challenging me to try it first. I did, sending the ball almost to half-court and pitying the small woman who would try to match that.

She did, of course, and more, using her arm as a lever and her entire body as a fulcrum, sending the ball flying away to the other end of the floor. Like all women I would come to know, she had secrets which, when revealed, would show me up.

At first, I believed the Babe Didrikson story she told, and then as I grew older and learned how to lie convincingly and defensively myself, I came to believe the story was at best an exaggeration and at worst an out-and-out fabrication. I learned well and early the use of fictitious narratives and depended upon their service. Decades later, though, my mother dead for over thirty years by then, I picked up a biography of Babe Didrikson in a library in Baltimore and flipped through it to the collection of photos at the center of the book. There beside Babe on both the basketball and volleyball teams, dressed in a uniform with a tie drawn up to the collar and long socks and strange athletic shoes, my mother stood looking out at me, her usual unsmiling serious self in a picture. Unlike her mythologizing son, she hadn't been lying after all.

Her husband, my father, Willie Ellis Duff, was six feet, five inches, in his stocking feet, and he reminded people of that fact all the time. He also was a handsome man, intelligent, and he spoke well and fulsomely, and those characteristics he asserted to any and all who would stand still to hear him, whether they were listening or not. He met my mother when they were both rooming in the home of Nelia Davis, an old lady in Nederland, a few miles south of Beaumont. Dorothy was attending nursing school at a hospital, and Willie was working as an oil field hand for a company somewhere in the area. Both were well past the usual age for unmarried men and women at the time, twenty-five for her and ten years older for him.

"First time I saw your mama, Gerald," he told me over and over (he told me all his stories, the same ones, throughout his life repeatedly, with the same amount of relish each time), "she was tripping up the steps of Nelia Davis's house there in Nederland, and I knew I had to meet her."

So in 1935 Dorothy Irwin, daughter of a respectable mid-level manager from the Midwest, married Willie Duff out of Polk County, deep in East Texas, the red clay of the failed family cotton farm heavy on his shoes. She settled for good and for ill in him and in all he ever was and did. Her family never understood the union, and neither did his.

What he crucially had in common with the woman he married, I think now, is that at age eleven both lost mothers, both had usurpers installed in their mothers' places by their fathers, and neither one ever accepted or understood the trauma that resulted. My mother's false mother was named Belle, and my father's was called Alice. Belle had children of her own, and so did Alice. The real difference between the two situations was the number of offspring involved. Dorothy's stepmother had a normal number of children of her own and produced no additional ones with her new husband John Irwin, and my grandfather Amos Duff, had thirteen children with my father's mother, proceeding to add nine more with Alice.

That second group, the half-brothers and half-sisters of my father and his true and full siblings, was always identified by them as "the top crop." I learned to consider that second harvest from Amos Duff's loins as beneath real consideration. They weren't of the same species as my father's real brothers and sisters, uncles Lewis and Jim and Miller and aunts Mary and Myrtle and Rosalie and MayBelle and Linnie and the other ones dead before I was born. The ones by Alice (I was taught never to call her grandmother or grandma but always Aunt Alice) had names like Effie and Dura and Ferguson and Yvonne and Valerie and Felder and other lesser ones whose names I never learned nor was expected to.

I also learned from my mother that I was to care about my aunts and my uncle on her side of the family, the Irwins, and I learned from my father and my mother to suspect, distrust, fear, despise, dismiss, ridicule, condemn, and criticize most of my father's true siblings and all of the "top crop," that whole collection of people from Polk County together named Duff and known by others throughout that country as the Duff bunch.

It made for double-mindedness in me and my sister Nancy. We were taught to admire and respect Aunt Ella, Aunt Norma and especially Uncle Roderick, the Irwins from Beaumont in Jefferson County, who had gone to real high schools and had come from Nebraska, one of those states far away and therefore cleaner and respectable and less emotionally cluttered than Texas. The Duffs, though, were a different breed. They never smiled or laughed or appeared to like seeing us unless they'd been drinking (always whiskey, straight from the bottle and never in a glass or in front of anybody else, expect for Uncle Lewis who'd drink anything anywhere at anytime and would come into his relatives' houses when they weren't home in his search for whiskey, which he would always find no matter how well it had been hidden). They didn't like each other ever and didn't mind showing it. In fact, they liked to say terrible things to each other about character flaws, wrong actions, and sorry behavior in their kin, in their kin's children, in-laws and acquaintances. And they did it often, and they did it well.

A good example was Pascal Richardson, the only child of Aunt Myrtle and Uncle Buck. Pascal had suffered polio at an early age, leaving his legs withered and useless, and he had to get around on crutches. Probably in reaction to the slowdown his disability caused him, Pascal developed a sharp tongue and a quick wit. He needed all the defenses he could come up with, given the fact that he lived with his parents on the hardscrabble cotton farm adjoining Aunt Mary's and Uncle Jesse's place with their six sons and one daughter. One day, the story went (and it was a story my father featured often in his arsenal of illustrations of sorriness in relatives and comeuppances duly dealt), Pascal found himself alone outside and undefended by an adult, with three or four of his first cousins ringed around him.

These three or four Richardson boys (they were double first cousins, their fathers brothers and their mothers sisters) were probably Jesse Lee, Bethel, and Wilson, and they immediately began to torment their crippled cousin, Pascal, mainly because he was there and it was possible to do so. *Why not?* My father always said when he was telling the story.

"I imagine Pascal had said something to one of them about the way he was dressed or looked or something he had done wrong in the schoolhouse, and that one took offense. Let's say it was Jesse Lee. He slipped up behind Pascal propped up there on his crutches mouthing off at that bunch and kicked one of the crutches loose to make Pascal fall. When he tumbled over, I expect all of them there in the side yard commenced to laugh and hooraw Pascal, and one of them got the idea to grab Pascal's crutches and throw them off in the weeds so he'd have to crawl to get them back while they stood there and laughed. Or maybe they figured they'd just run off and leave Pascal by himself to get his crutches back and have to try to catch up with them but not be able to.

"Anyway, Jesse Lee knocked that crutch loose and Pascal fell over, but the mistake Jesse Lee made, see, was that he didn't make sure he got both crutches loose from Pascal at the same time. You understand that Pascal is all muscled up in his arms and chest and shoulders. You know why that is, Gerald?"

I told him yes I did, since I'd heard the story numerous times by then, and I proceeded to explain the compensation in upper body strength Pascal had achieved since he'd lost all force in his legs. But Willie Duff didn't wait for me to demonstrate what I knew about the subject. He just kept talking, because it pleased him to do that. Always. Once begun, a story had to be finished. The laws of narrative demanded completion.

"Pascal couldn't run and catch one of them boys bothering him, but he could use that other crutch, and by God, he did. Know what he did?"

"No," I said, giving up and letting the narrative flow. "What?"

"When Jesse Lee ran up to grab that loose crutch, the one he'd knocked out from under Pascal, Pascal reared back there on the ground where he was lying in among the grass burrs and caught Jesse Lee just above the right eye with the end of that crutch he still had. Knocked him colder than a wedge, too. Then when Bethel started running for the house to get his mama to come see what a terrible thing Pascal had done to his brother, Pascal slung that crutch like a spear and nailed Bethel in the back of the head and sent him winding."

"What did Wilson do?" I said, taking up my expected role in the dialogue.

"He started squalling like a schoolgirl and run for the house. And it was a lucky damn thing for him that Pascal didn't have a third crutch or he'd a laid Wilson out, too, before he got out of range."

The first time I told this story of Pascal among the double first cousins to somebody outside my family, it was to a girl I was trying to impress, expecting her to respond the same way my sisters, cousins, uncles, and aunts always did when they heard the tale. My family always viewed it as a sermon on the danger of messing with a crippled man who was muscled up in the shoulders and arms, able to use his crutches as weapons, and not be defeated simply because he'd been rendered flat on his back in among a patch of grass burrs.

"The poor boy," the girl I was regaling said. "What kind of animals would torment a disabled person on crutches? They should've been put in jail."

"No," I said, trying to express the Duff family perspective. "Pascal did all right. He laid out two of them and would have turned Wilson a flip, too, if he could've got to the other crutch. But he couldn't crawl to it while Wilson was still in range."

She still didn't understand the point of the story and what the Duff bunch valued in it, of course, not being of the tribe herself. We Duffs weren't worried about Pascal, there in the grass burrs with both crutches out of reach, or about Jesse Lee, slowly coming to with a big knot on his forehead, or with Bethel, nailed from behind by a crutch thrown by his disabled double first cousin. They all got what they deserved, including Pascal, we knew without thinking about it, and the only thing wrong with the event was that Wilson got away unscathed. My father, the uncle of the whole lot of them, would have loved the symmetry of the story if Wilson had gotten his fair share of punishment, too.

On one occasion of my father's telling of this particular Pascal story (there were other ones, too, mainly about Pascal's mistreatment of his mother and the demands for attention and special favors he put on her and Uncle Buck, but the crutch one was the best in my opinion), I asked my father what happened then after Pascal had nailed Jesse Lee and Bethel and Wilson had run off.

"What did Pascal do next?" I said, "After that?"

"I don't know," my father said peevishly. "I expect he crawled over to his crutches and got up on them and run to Myrtle a-crying about how bad he'd been treated."

"Did he?"

"I don't know, I told you. It was over by then," my father said, knowing instinctively what Aristotle did about the beginning, middle, and end of a narrative, and ready to go on to the next account of some East Texas action brought to his mind by association of ideas. My mother would have wanted to speak about aftermaths, but Willie Duff nailed the truth about the way a story should work, as though he were launching a crutch himself and had reached his target. Once well and truly hit, the target was no longer of interest, whether it was Jesse Lee Richardson's head or the crux of a narrative.

CHAPTER 3

The War in Texas

I WAS AFRAID A GOOD BIT OF THE TIME IN MY CHILDHOOD, AS I REMEMBER, BUT that didn't worry me. It was usual. The war with the Japs was there, and I came to consciousness of myself and the place where I found myself located with the war as a steady presence and as expected and inevitable as the winter rain on the Texas Gulf Coast. I watched all airplanes that flew over the house, asking my mother if they were Jap or ours and particularly if they might be carrying Uncle Miller on his way to fight the Japs. At first she would tell me the planes couldn't all be carrying Miller Duff, but after having to endure the same questions from me about each aircraft that appeared, she finally gave up and said *all* of them had my uncle as a passenger.

I knew we were fighting the Germans as well as the Japanese, but I wasn't really afraid of the Germans the way I was of the yellow, slant-eyed, bucktoothed little men I saw in cartoons in the magazines my father read. These publications had names like *Argosy* and *Man* and *Warrior*, but the greatest of these was the magazine called *True*. What it presented was real, it said so on the front cover, and my father believed that. He read me the stories within, the true ones about Japanese torturing American soldiers and about snakes as big as a man swallowing children and tigers in India roaming from house to house looking for live meat.

I learned from *True*, as I leaned over my father's shoulder to listen to what he was reading to me, the smell from him a mixture of aftershave lotion, tobacco, and my father's own particular scent: the world was filled with paralyzing danger. One false move and you were chewed up, poisoned by venom, or drowned by bucktoothed Jap soldiers wearing thick glasses.

Not only did *True Magazine* bring the truth into our house, but an actual captured Japanese midget sub was put on display in downtown Beaumont, across from the Jefferson Theatre, and my parents took me to see it. I was eager to go until we actually got there and joined the line of people waiting to see the submarine which the government was sending all over the country to encourage the terrified populace to buy war bonds. I learned that fact later from a documentary on PBS about Pearl Harbor and the uses to which the midget Japanese sub captured there in 1941 was put, but at the time I viewed the sub in Beaumont I assumed it had been operating just off the beach south of Sabine Pass, Texas, not twenty miles from the Jefferson Theatre on Pearl Street.

So as I climbed up the ramp to peer into the innards of the Japanese killing machine, I was already having serious second thoughts about the prospect. When I was lifted up by my father to look into the open hatch of the conning tower, I was unprepared for what my horrified eyes told me. Not only was I seeing into the guts of the tiny craft, but I was also seeing people. The Jap crew was in there, both of them, dressed in their strange greenish uniforms, wearing their thick glasses as they leaned forward to operate the controls of their craft from hell, aiming their deadly torpedoes at Texas, where I lived. I knew if I waited too long to get away from my perch over the conning tower that one or both of them would look up, identify me for the victim they craved and through some foreign war-loving magic, would be appearing in my bedroom that very night.

I expect I screamed, of course, as I always did when confronted with what I feared and knew would get me in some way before too long, and I fought to free myself from my father's arms and escape. I do remember the laughter and jeers of the crowd of people around me as they pointed to the boy too scared to face the reality of the Japanese crew among us in Beaumont, and I remember listening to my mother explain over and over again that the little buck-toothed yellow men I saw in the midget sub were not real Japs at all, but dummies dressed up in captured uniforms.

"What are they made of?" I remember asking. "If they're dummies? Why is one of them looking through the periscope if he's not real? I could see him breathing. He was drawing in air and letting it out. Dummies can't do that, can they?"

"Oh, yes," she said, "Dummies can do anything now, the way they make them to work."

That claim by my mother was even more terrifying to me, as I contemplated Jap dummies, not even real men, finding their way into my bedroom, the eyes behind their thick glasses dead and mechanical and as unfeeling as those of the jeering crowd on Pearl Street in Beaumont. "Can they move, then?" I asked. "Can they move and get around on their feet? On their own?"

"Yes," she told me in ignorance of what I feared most, "they're made of some kind of clay, and the people who made them have got it fixed so the Jap dummies can move. That's all there is to it. They're not real, Gerald."

The dreams I had from hearing that lasted me the rest of World War II, and well into my adolescence. The notion of something unliving, yet able to move against me unmotivated by intent, represented the depth of horror to me.

Somewhere around that time I began to bite my fingernails, I remember, and to stutter like a machine gun when I tried to speak. Discovering the comfort of fingernail-biting was what got me through the succession of nights that attended each day of that part of my childhood, though, and I was glad I had myself to chew on and occupy my mind.

My father tolerated his son's stuttering, but the fingernail-biting was wholly unacceptable to Big Willie Duff out of Polk County, Texas. I overheard him and my mother discussing the matter once as I lay in my bed with the light on (the light had to be on in my room for the duration of the aftermath of the midget sub episode), and my mother was attempting to explain to her husband why this sissy nail-biting continued despite all threats and prohibitions against it.

"Willie," she was saying, "Gerald bites his fingernails because he's nervous."

"Nervous," Big Willie said. "Nervous? My little brother Miller is over there in the Pacific fighting the goddamn Japs in the islands, and he doesn't bite his fingernails. Miller's not nervous. What the hell has Gerald got to be nervous about?"

I lay there in the well-lit bedroom, careful to keep all of my body in the middle of the bed so that no part of any arm or hand or foot could hang over the edge where it could be detected by a thing under the bed lying in wait for just such a chance, and I knew to my core just what I had to be nervous about. I chewed my nails until my fingers bled, and that helped some. My main worry on an ongoing basis was not whether to chew or not chew, but about how long a time my nails were in growing back enough for my teeth to get a good purchase on what was left.

I didn't worry about America's other enemy, the Germans, though. I had seen German soldiers in person already by that time, and they had posed no threat. It happened while my mother and I were waiting for a bus on the side of the road to Beaumont, the Twin City Highway, in Nederland where we had moved by then. Far up the road, I spotted an open truck approaching, its bed filled with men standing packed together, all dressed alike in what I remember as light gray clothes. As they neared, a couple of them waved and I waved back, and by the time the truck passed us, all of the men in the bed of the truck were waving and grinning at me and my mother. I waved harder, until suddenly my mother grabbed my hand and pulled it down to her side.

"Don't wave at them, Gerald," she said. "For goodness sakes, that's a bunch of German prisoners."

I wasn't surprised by her saying that, having learned to accept that anything might happen at any point on any given day where I lived—tigers at large, things beneath my bed, midget subs on display complete with crew, German prisoners riding by in an open truck—but I was disappointed in having my relationship with the men in the truck cut off so abruptly. It wasn't often that some stranger noticed me enough to let me know that fact, and to have a whole truckload of blond-haired men wearing the same kind of clothes do so and to show friendly appreciation about it was gratifying.

Years later I realized that the German prisoners of war were probably waving at an attractive woman standing by the side of the road and hadn't even noticed there was a child beside her. But being told at the time that the friendly wavers were Germans was a real boon to me. I gathered from the experience that I didn't have to worry about Germans in all those long nights ahead of me as I did about the yellow men called Japs by all the grown-ups around me. Germans soldiers wouldn't sneak into my room under the cover of darkness as the Japanese would. Germans rode by in trucks in gray clothes, smiling and waving at little boys on the highway.

I was relieved. I had my hands full already with the Japanese, and reassured by the episode with the German prisoners of war being hauled off that morning from their camp to work in the rice fields of the Texas Gulf Coast (though I didn't know that then), I could concentrate on thinking about the yellow-skinned torturers who traveled around in midget submarines. That, along with Bengal tigers and giant anacondas, was work enough to keep me occupied.

I did make fictive use later of the fact that German prisoners of war were kept in that part of Texas, though. It happened one morning when my mother had had to leave me and my sister Nancy with my Aunt Linnie while she went to Beaumont for a doctor's appointment. Aunt Linnie and Uncle Arnold lived two houses down from us in Nederland, and she had come to our place that day rather than having us in hers. She did that probably for the chance to rummage in mother's chifforobe and chest of drawers to see what she could find. Aunt Linnie was bad to do that, and in fact most of the Duff bunch would come into the empty houses of other family members at any opportunity to look around for what they might discover and on occasions walk off with.

My mother was expert at detecting when someone else had been in her house uninvited, and I remember many times her complaining to my father after we had arrived back home from an absence, brief as it might have been.

"Willie," she'd say, throwing doors open and slamming clothes hangers together until they jangled. "Lewis has been in here looking in the closets for whiskey."

Or, "Willie, I swear I had some pictures in the top drawer of this bed table, and now they're gone. One of your sisters has come in here and taken those two of me and Gerald at the carnival."

"That'd be Linnie," my father would say. "She's the one that steals pictures. Rosalie will go to the ice box and take bacon or a roast. Meat's what she's generally after."

But that morning my mother had to take the bus into Beaumont to see the doctor, and she had no choice of where Aunt Linnie would be willing to watch me and Nancy. So that's where my aunt was, in our living room coiled up in an overstuffed chair, questioning me closely about the activities and habits of my mama and daddy, Nancy at play on the floor with some small object. An empty medicine bottle, maybe, or a spoon or picture book. Whatever it was, I remember scrawling on it with a Crayola at some point, not enough to goad my sister into a complete breakdown, but sufficient to generate a cry or two of outrage and anguish. Enough to satisfy me, certainly, and to cause Aunt Linnie to glare at me over the top of her glasses.

"Gerald," she said. "Be still and let me ask you something."

"Yes, ma'am," I said. "What?" I liked questions usually. They gave me a chance to speak to someone who appeared to be listening, at least for the duration of my answer, though their attention rapidly began to fade when I began to stutter. Seeing them lose interest made the problem I had speaking worse, of course, and I would speed up my rate of speech to get as much out as possible before I seized up completely in my voice apparatus. But this time my Aunt Linnie seemed ready to listen to me as long as I wanted to talk. There was something she wanted to hear.

"Do your mama and daddy ever talk mean to each other, Gerald?" she said, now looking directly at me through her lenses, her eyes magnified at least twofold.

"When?" I said. "You mean when they're arguing?"

"That's just exactly what I'm talking about. When they're arguing. What do they argue about, your mama and daddy?"

"Nothing," I said. "They just argue."

"What do they say? That's what I'm talking about. Do they ever talk about me?"

"No."

"Yes," Nancy said from the floor. "Mama and Daddy do talk about Aunt Linnie. Yes, they do."

"No, they don't, Nancy," I said. "They never say her name."

"They do, too. They say 'oh Lord here comes Linnie.'"

"That's what I figured," Aunt Linnie said. "Here she comes, huh?"

"Nancy," I said, talking fast because I could feel my words getting away from me, so fast they were about to run into each other and blow up like a hand grenade thrown by a Japanese soldier in the jungle. "Shut up."

At that my sister began to whine, and Aunt Linnie leaned forward to speak to her. I remember she patted Nancy on the head, but she was looking at me the whole time. "You know what to say when Gerald tells you to shut up?"

"No," Nancy said, close now to full outcry. "What?"

"Whenever he says something mean to you like shut up, you just say, 'I don't shut up, I grow up, and when I look at you I throw up.'"

"When she says that," I managed to squeeze out of my rapidly collapsing voice box, "I just say 'you're crazy, Nancy.'"

"When he says 'you're crazy, Sugar,'" Aunt Linnie said, "you just say, 'if I'm crazy, you're nuts, I eat the chicken, you eat the guts.'"

I knew where my aunt got that one. From Willie Vee, her daughter. And I had memorized the response that was called for to that, but my ability to speak had by then completely abandoned me. All I could do was run out of the room down the hall into my mother's and father's bedroom, thinking of the thing I wished I could say back but couldn't. "Yeah, and I'll take them chicken guts and put them on a hook and catch me a fish to eat. That's a whole lot better than chicken, fish is." That didn't rhyme, but it was something to say back. Saying the right words could save you and put you on top, and I had gotten that fact by heart early on.

My problem at the moment was Aunt Linnie, I realized, but I knew there was no way I could get to her. She was a grown-up, and therefore untouchable, ache though I did to see her in hell with her back broke, as Willie Duff would say of those who annoyed him. My sister was there, though, and she was all I had to resort to. I would make her pay for the treatment I'd just received from the woman reared up on the couch in our living room coaching Nancy on ways to get back at me.

So I did what I always did when I was in my parents' bedroom alone. I started rummaging through the dressing table drawers, choosing that over the chifforobe since nothing ever changed in that piece of furniture. It held my mother's dresses, an ironed shirt or two of my father's, some pairs of shoes, nothing of much interest, though it was big enough to hide in with the door closed. I used that space from time to time.

The dressing table with its three mirrors which allowed you to see all sides of yourself if you jerked your head around fast enough had some small drawers, the contents of which did change now and then by an item or two. No such luck for me that morning, though. But I did find a bottle of aspirin, whose top was loosely fastened enough for me to twist off. Immediately I saw what I must do, removed one of the tablets, and took off for the kitchen. I could hear Aunt Linnie grilling Nancy in the living room and Nancy heaving her guts under interrogation in a way I had learned not to do. But I also knew my sister didn't know much anyway, so there was no advantage to be gained by my eavesdropping for a tidbit I could reveal to my mother as having been dropped by Nancy to Aunt Linnie. Who cared what the new kittens had been named?

I could reach a paring knife in a cabinet drawer, there was an apple in a bowl on the table, and in less than a minute I had carved out a plug and replaced it so that you could hardly tell anything had been done unless you knew about it. Before I replaced the plug in the hole I'd dug in the apple, I bit off its tip and put the aspirin beneath it. The surprise was ready.

Aunt Linnie didn't like the fact I had an apple from my own kitchen in my hand when I entered the living room. I should have asked her permission to take it, of course, but I could tell what she was going to do about that violation before I even came into the room. Tell? I was counting on it.

"Give Nancy that apple, Gerald," my aunt told me. "Let her have a bite out of it first before you start gnawing on it."

So I did, without protest, carefully turning the piece of fruit so Nancy bit into just the right spot. It seemed to me at the time that it took a while before my little sister began sputtering and crying about the bad taste of the apple, though it was probably only a few seconds. But as soon as she got a healthy dose of the aspirin, crying out that the apple tasted bad, like medicine, as she put it, I knew all hell was about to break loose in that little house on Detroit Street in Nederland, Texas.

My body knew it, too, and I instantly had to pee, visualizing myself breaking for the outhouse in the backyard, but not being allowed to do that by the express command of Aunt Linnie.

"Stay right where you are, Gerald," she said, the apple in her hand as she peered through her glasses at the dissolved white material in Nancy's bite mark. "Did you get any of this poison in your mouth? Answer me, boy. Don't stand there just a-sputtering."

"No," I told her, grabbing my pee-pee so the wet wouldn't come out and get on my pants. "Why do you think it's poison in that apple. I bet it ain't."

"I know poison when I see it," Aunt Linnie said, sniffing at the apple in her hand. "Oh, Lord have mercy, it smells like a chemical. How much did she get in her mouth, Gerald?"

"Not hardly any. Not enough to count a bit. I bet if Nancy drank some water, she'd be just fine."

"She can't drink water, you little idiot. That'll drive the poison right into her system, and she'll be dead in three minutes."

"Look, Aunt Linnie," I said, my wee-wee demanding exit as I stood in one spot, jiggling up and down. All the colors in the room had become glaringly bright, I noticed, dark and rainy as it still was outside. "We have been missing aspirins around here. I heard mama talking about it. Let me count how many we got in the bottle and see if one is gone."

I remember thinking at the time that if she did count our aspirins and agree we'd come up short one that I'd have a lot of trouble making up a convincing story as to why I knew the count of aspirins was so crucial in our household and that an inventory was maintained about the supply on a regular basis. That, though, I'd figure out later. Right now I had to offer up the truth told slant about what Nancy had bitten into, or the situation would get a whole lot worse a lot quicker. Things were fixing to get completely out of control, and I marveled to myself about how fast bad stuff could grow worse even as you watched it happen. This one was a doozy.

Aunt Linnie was coming apart before my eyes, and her usual suspicious nature, quick to seize on any clue left by a guilty child no matter how small or insignificant to the ordinary eye, would lead her invariably to the truth. She was a master of inquisition, and by mentioning an aspirin lack in the Duff household I had handed her on a platter all she needed to know to ferret out the truth about what I had been up to. Why wouldn't she see what a liar I was being?

But she didn't take what I had given her. It was as though I hadn't even mentioned aspirin, so I tried it again. "I really think there's at least one, maybe two aspirins, missing from the bottle in Mama and Daddy's room," I said, and then inspired by Aunt Linnie's early interest in what my parents argued about, I went on.

"I heard Mama and Daddy arguing about it last night," I said. "They were saying you know I think there's an aspirin gone out of that bottle, and Mama was trying to make Daddy believe you'd took it, Aunt Linnie. Yeah, Mama said, 'I expect Linnie came in here while I was at the grocery store and stole an aspirin or two out of the bottle. She must have popped that stick loose out of the window where I had it propped so nobody could open it up and crawl into the house. Linnie did that. Came right over that window sill.'"

Getting all that out was a burden, given my stutter which had reached a level that morning that astounded even me, but I worked at it until every word had been uttered, some of them forty or fifty times. Aunt Linnie was not buying it.

"This ain't no aspirin, Gerald," she said. "Shut up and open your mouth real wide so I can look in it."

It was at that point my mother came through the front door, back from the doctor's office in Beaumont, and she recognized disaster when she saw it. "Mama," I said, "I got to go pee-pee, and I think there's an aspirin missing. I been counting them ever since you left the house."

"What?" my mother said. "What's happened to Nancy? Why's Gerald standing with his mouth wide open like that?"

"Germans," Aunt Linnie said. "I done figured it out. It came to me. It makes perfect sense. Them German prisoners are poisoning the produce on the farms yonder out Koolemay Road, and Nancy has got hold of a apple just plumb full of chemicals. Smell this thing, Dorothy. It'll make you want to puke just sniffing it."

At my mother's entrance, Nancy's squalling reached a new high, the pitch of her screams so elevated I stopped hearing it for a second or two. "Mama," I said. "Listen to me about this missing aspirin out of that bottle in y'all's bedroom. I believe I got it figured out." That's what I was trying to say at least, but neither of the grown women in the room wanted to listen.

"Get some water warmed up, Linnie," my mother was saying, throwing what she was carrying to the floor, sweeping Nancy up and heading for the kitchen sink. "I'll mix dry mustard and ipecac in a glass and make both of them vomit it up. By the time Dr. Weisbach gets here, they'll both be dead unless we do something."

At that, I broke and ran for the outside, but Aunt Linnie was quick on her feet in those days and had me pinioned under her left arm before I even got to the door. The mixture of mustard and ipecac tasted worse than I thought it would and it got the job done quickly and well. Nancy and I stood side by side on the back porch, puking onto the ground where the drip from the eaves had made crater patterns in the gravel, and I watched my breakfast fall into a map of a place I'd never seen before. I knew I had to drop the aspirin story now, the budding editor in me realizing its current irrelevance because of the passage of events. If they ever realized I was the source of the "chemical" in Nancy's apple and not some scheming German prisoner of war working on the government farm by day and poisoning produce by night, the gastric suffering I was going through would be nothing up beside what a switch from the willow in our backyard would do to my butt and the backs of my bare legs.

So I never mentioned the event again to anybody, not even my mother, though I had considered telling her the truth years later. I finally decided to let her die innocent of that, sparing her having to take one more of her son's lies to the grave with her. Instead I published an account of the episode in a short story in a literary magazine when I was teaching at Vanderbilt, effectively burying the truth for good. Who reads those things and the kind of stuff that's in them, anyway? It's all just fiction, and the symbolic use of the apple is pitifully transparent.

CHAPTER 4

The Cat and Dog Picture Shows

WHILE WE WERE LIVING IN NEDERLAND BEFORE I STARTED SCHOOL, MY FATHER worked days at the Sun Oil Company, which would eventually fire him for getting too old for manual labor. Once or twice a month my mother used to take me with her to Beaumont on the bus for shopping, or going to the doctor, and these trips always involved taking in a movie at the Jefferson or Liberty and having lunch at the counter in Kresge's, the biggest dime store in the city. I don't remember Nancy's being with us, and if I had thought about it at the time, I would have been glad she wasn't.

I wanted the experience of eating a Kresge's toasted ham sandwich and drinking a Coke from a glass to be mine alone, not even to speak of walking into the lobby of the Jefferson Theater and stroking the legs of the naked statues of men and women set into niches cut into the walls. Years later, I realized the 1920s movie palace that was the Jefferson had been conceived and built with a classical theme in mind, but when I first encountered it I simply accepted that naked ladies with their breasts exposed and men with leaves over their pee-pees were regulation movie house furniture. I didn't know why they arranged things that way, but I was glad they did.

I don't remember any part of any of the movies I saw as I sat beside my mother in the Jefferson Theater at that time. I remember the way things smelled, the way the plush seat felt against my bare legs, the nipples on the naked stone ladies, the huge marble urinals in the restroom, the fact my mother didn't want to talk to me during the movie, and the way the silver light from the screen looked washing over the profile of her face as she sat beside me.

She didn't seem real at those moments, and I wondered during each movie projected who she was, this lady beside me, and whether she'd turn back into my mother again after *The End* came up on the screen this time. What if she didn't? What if that woman was gone forever, and I'd have to find a way to live with this new one?

Though I was always glad to enter the lobby of the Jefferson with my own ticket in hand, by the end of each picture show I was glad to walk out of the darkness and into the glare and heat of the sun outside the lobby, the sidewalk beneath my feet hard, gritty, and spotted with spit-out wads of chewing gum melted into it forever. Here was the real thing, and the woman holding my hand was the same mother that put me on the bus in Nederland, brought me to Beaumont, and took me back home. Pretty pictures in the dark were fun, but I wanted my fountain Coke and my toasted ham sandwich.

Something that happened once in the Jefferson reinforced my growing sense in my pre-school years that it was impossible to predict what would upset my mother (or my father, for that matter), what would get me deeply in trouble, and what would simply be a passing irritation to her, of no more consequence than the rain showers that came every day on summer afternoons on the Gulf Coast. You couldn't go outside without getting soaked, but half an hour after the rain stopped things were as hot as ever.

I forget what picture show was playing that day, probably one of those that involved lots of scenes of a man and woman staring at each other until they kissed and then arguing in loud voices afterward, but it was one that didn't touch me. I was bored enough that I finally began to beg my mother to let me go to the restroom by myself, something I knew was hopeless since she never let me go into the men's but always took me into the women's when she went. The movie must have been one that engaged her, though, because she finally told me to go ahead and come straight back.

In the Jefferson Theatre's men's room, the most impressive sight for me was always the urinals, huge stone vaults into which you aimed your pee-pee, as it was politely called in my family. So that day I stood before one of these monuments, ready to let go, and it came to me that it would be interesting to pee-pee instead on the floor in front of the urinal in defiance of what a man was expected to do. Why not do that? It might splash up in a different and new way.

It did, and that pleased me, right up to the point where my arm was grabbed by an usher in the blue and red uniform of the Jefferson Theatre. He asked me why I was doing that when it was clear that the urinal was right in front of me. I remember in the days after that humiliation that I thought of things I might have said to him, explanations that would have made him apologize for bothering me and for escorting me back to my mother and telling her what I'd done.

I'm a little blind boy, I could have said, and I can't tell where I'm aiming my pee-pee. But that one would have been hard to pull off, since I didn't have the glasses for it. I was afraid I'd fall in, I could have claimed, appealing to his sympathy for a boy so small. The thing was, he didn't look, sound, or act sympathetic as he jerked me along beside him, the beam of his big flashlight pointing the way to where my mother sat watching a couple of people kissing on the silver screen.

I finally settled in my days of thoughtful revision after the deed was done, accomplished, over, unchangeable, on this notion. What if I had said, "All right. I did it. I'm not going to try to tell you a story. But here. . . ." At that point going to the pocket of my short pants, "Here's a dime for your trouble. That ought to even us up."

Then I could have zipped my pants, sauntered back into the auditorium, pausing to caress the stone calf of one of the female statues in its niche in the wall of the Jefferson, and sat back down by my mother, who would have been none the wiser for what I'd just accomplished.

I had learned the power of money already by then, and I have regretted ever since that I didn't have that dime to buy off the Jefferson Theatre cop. Instead, I had to stand beside my mother as the man in uniform lit me up with the beam of his flashlight and listen to him squeal about what I'd just done in the marble restroom of the picture show. I don't remember exactly how my mother responded, though I do know she went back to watching the show in progress as I sat slumped beside her not even looking up at the giant faces locked in conversation and kisses.

For once, though, I didn't have to pay for my crime later, or at least I don't remember suffering any corporal punishment or having to endure my mother relating to my father what Gerald had done today in the Jefferson Theatre. After I was married and had children of my own, it came to me finally that my mother probably didn't care to let my father know she had gone to the picture show in Beaumont that day. She let me off because she was hiding something, too.

Most of my lies to my parents were in the service of self-protection, but the ones I told my sister Nancy came out of my wanting things to be true that weren't. I personally always knew when I was lying about something, since I had better sense than to believe the things I made up, but my sister was truly gullible. And I've always appreciated her for that, from then up to now.

Nancy's belief in what I told her, no matter how outrageously preposterous each of my remakings of reality happened to be at the moment, made me think they might be possible. It could be true, for example, that our cats and dogs, big and little, grown-ups and puppies and kittens, at the end of each day of lolling about the yard and eating scraps and drinking water and sleeping in the sun could begin to change at twilight. Why not? Wouldn't they like to try something different at night? I knew I would.

"Nancy," I told her on many occasions. "Do you know what the cats and dogs around here do at night after we've all gone to sleep in the house?"

"No," she'd say, speaking around the thumb she'd just popped into her mouth to get ready to listen to me spin my tale. "You mean the kittens, too?"

"All of them," I'd say. "Yep, they all like to get together in that little house in the backyard."

We would both turn and look at the old chicken house, converted somewhere along the way into a shed where our mother kept boxes of jelly jars and canning materials. "Right there," I'd say. "That's where it all happens."

By that point, Nancy had fallen into silent communion with her thumb, and I'd fill in the details of my revelation of the antics of the Duff family animals out on the town after dark. "They all get dressed up in clothes once it's nighttime, shirts and pants, shoes, hats, everything they need to put on so they can go to the picture show. Tommy is the one who runs the light that makes the pictures come out and get on the wall."

Tommy was the oldest dog in the menagerie and best able to handle machinery, I was prepared to argue, though Nancy never asked for supporting evidence. "They go out there to the little house, all of them dressed up, and see the cat and dog picture shows almost every night."

"Not when it's raining," Nancy would say at this point.

"Not usually. Sometimes, though, when it's a special show, they will go in the rain to their theater. They'll use umbrellas to stay dry."

"What kind of special show?" she'd ask.

"Cowboys. Like when a tomcat dresses up like Gene Autry in the picture show."

"Oh," she'd say, and go back to her thumb, and I'd know the thrill of an audience satisfied.

I don't remember Nancy as a child ever telling anyone else what I'd revealed to her about the picture-show viewing habits of our dogs and cats, but in all the years of our adulthood, she's been delighted to be able to let other people know what I used to tell her. And in my presence, of course. To her, the story reveals a dark side of me evident even in my early years, a propensity to utter that which is not so, a willingness to make up stuff, to mislead, to tell lies and to swear to the truth of them to the bitter end.

Generally these days when my sister informs whoever she happens to be addressing about our youth together, I smile and nod and agree, the affable big brother caught out finally in my childhood web of deceit. Once in a while, I'll deny ever having told Nancy such tales, though, and that will bring her to anger and at times to tears.

"Nancy's always making things up about those days," I'll say, doing it again to my sister, lying about plain and simple truth in a way designed to make her look foolish. And she'll rage and go dark in the face, and look at me in contempt and later ask my wife why I persist in being the way I am. Why can't her brother just take life as it is?

"Don't you wish it had been true, Nancy?" I asked her once in the aftermath of my lying as an adult about my lying as a child. "Wouldn't it have been wonderful if the dogs and cats, big and little, had gone to picture shows in our backyard, all dressed up in clothes like we wore and watched movies with dogs and cats playing all the parts? Wouldn't you have liked that?"

"That's crazy, Gerald," she said, standing before me with a look of triumph.

"It didn't happen, so it *couldn't* happen. Dogs and cats are just dogs and cats. They are now, and they were then, and they always will be."

And this from a woman who believes so deeply and purely in the bonds of blood between parents and children, brothers and sisters and cousins and uncles and aunts, despite having grown up as a member of that Duff bunch. I wasn't satisfied with the way the world was when I was a child, so I found a way to revise it. So has my sister in her adult years, according to a separate formulation. She prefers a faith in family ties. I liked cats and dogs watching picture shows on the silver screen of a reimagined chicken coop. Which vision is more real? Nancy knows, but I don't.

CHAPTER 5

The Calves of Dolly Roberts's Legs

It was midmorning, and I was lying across Dolly Roberts's bed, trying to understand why I was enjoying so much looking at the calves of Dolly's legs as she lolled on her stomach reading a magazine. Dolly was probably about nineteen or so, married to a young man named J.D. Roberts, who worked at the Sun Oil Company with my father, and Dolly was keeping me while my mother was gone somewhere. Ordinarily, I would have been protesting hotly about being left behind by my mother, but being on the same bed with Dolly as she let her bare feet wave back and forth while she read her magazine was strangely satisfying to me.

I knew my enjoyment had to be wrong. It was too intense not to be, and the fact that being on the bed with Dolly made me not care about my mother's absence was a sure sign I was up to something unapproved. What, I didn't know, but I suspected it was of the same family as the trouble I had gotten into for tearing out a magazine ad showing a woman leaning over a spring pouring water from a vase or jug. She had no clothes on the top part of her body, and what little she had beneath her waist was filmy, almost transparent. Her breasts were what drew my eye, though, and it was for them I had torn the page out of the magazine and stuck it in my shirt pocket. Every once in a while on the day I had done that, I'd take the picture out of my pocket for another look.

When I did, the look didn't satisfy me, and that was strange, so I'd put the picture back where I kept it for safekeeping, knowing full well I'd be feeling the need to take another look at the breasts of the lady with the container of water in her hand any time now. I wanted to see it, to study her breasts, to determine if I could see through her filmy robe covering the lower part of whatever was hidden there, but there was no ultimate satisfaction in my looking at the picture. But I couldn't stop thinking about doing it, and I couldn't stop doing it.

It wasn't unusual for me to put pieces of paper or bits of string or pebbles or bottle caps and assorted other pieces of trash in my pockets, particularly after I started Nederland Elementary School. I'd spot something on the ground, be seized with the notion that whatever it was I'd picked out for pity had been separated from its own kind and cast in with unfeeling and unfriendly strangers. Feeling a deep sympathy with the article of trash before me, I'd pick it up for safekeeping, intending to give it a loving and secure home as soon as I got back to my house.

My mother would often ask me why I kept sticking such useless items in my pockets, and I'd profess ignorance of their being where she'd found them or I'd try to find some other way to lie about what I'd intended, and the topic would be dropped. That was true ordinarily, but not with the painting of the naked lady bending over and showing her wonderfully tantalizing breasts. That one my mother did not take in stride. She explained to me that what I'd done was *nasty*, as she put it. She said I should never do it again and that I should never look at pictures of naked ladies in the future, and she promised to wear me out if she discovered I was doing so again.

So that was wrong, looking at certain bare parts of women's bodies, despite my inability to break myself of the desire to do so, and the pleasure I derived from watching Dolly Roberts's feet move lazily back and forth as she lolled on her bed near me that morning was forbidden, secret, and not to be acknowledged or revealed.

Finally, Dolly noticed my steady staring and looked up from her magazine. "What are you looking at so hard, Gerald?" she said in a voice I recognized as playful. "Are you noticing how dirty my feet are?"

"No," I swore, fearful I'd been found out. "I'm not looking at your feet. I'm not looking at anything. I'm just resting my eyes."

"Well, let me get up and make you some toast," I remember her saying. "Maybe you're hungry this time of morning."

Ordinarily I would have jumped at the chance she'd offered at something to eat off-schedule, but if she left the bed we were sharing, I knew I'd lose my view of her calves waving back and forth slowly before me. "No, Dolly," I said. "You just keep reading your book, and I'll let my eyes rest some more."

At that, Dolly laughed, jumped up and headed for the toaster, and I knew that somehow I'd given myself away again to a woman's superior intelligence.

The first verbal reference to that whole dark relationship between males and females I encountered in the backyard of our house next door to Dolly's and J.D.'s, and it came from a boy a couple of years older than I was. One day Kenwood Delcambre asked me if I knew what the word *fuck* meant. I didn't, but I immediately realized I wanted and needed to know, and that it was a bit of information I'd never hear from my mother and one that I'd have to keep from her. Something about the sound of the word let me know it was powerful and forbidden and *nasty*, and I was dying to learn all I could about it.

"No, Kenwood," I admitted. "I don't know what fuck means. Tell me."

"It means," Kenwood said, looking around him to be sure no grown-up was in range, "it means, *fuck* does, this thing right here I'm going to tell you. It means the racer through the tunnel."

"A racer?"

"Yeah, Gerald. A racing car going through a tunnel. That's what *fuck* means. Don't tell nobody you heard it from me."

I never did, though I didn't understand what Kenwood Delcambre meant exactly, but the image of a small, brightly colored racing car zipping through a dark tunnel seized my imagination instantly, and I thought about the picture it created off and on for weeks. Why was it so exciting, I wondered. Why was it something I could never mention to my mother? Why were Dolly Roberts's legs mixed up with it? Why did I never say the word *fuck* to my mother, as my sister Nancy did a couple of years later when some girl printed it on a piece of paper torn from a Big Chief tablet and gave it to Nancy to keep? Why did I know the power and allure the word had, when all I knew about it was that racing cars and tunnels characterized it for Kenwood Delcambre?

I couldn't answer those questions, but I knew permanently at age five that I'd have to deal with what that word meant from then on. And I was ready to do it, whatever it took. I would study it, I would try to figure it out, and I would make up stories about it from then on out. Maybe I could make it understandable if I lied enough about it. I pledged that to myself then, and I'm still writing fiction about people trying to live with and make sense of that mystery Kenwood Delcambre introduced me to those years ago.

CHAPTER 6

The Brass Knucks in Mama's Dresser

Along about that same time when we were living in the house on Detroit Street in Nederland, I was awakened late one night by the sound of a grown man crying. The sounds weren't soft, and they weren't expressions from someone who'd only had his feelings hurt. The sobs were loud, they were full of pain, and they had blood in them.

When I got to the scene, I could see that the crying was being done by my father's first cousin Ernest Duff, and he was holding out one hand toward my mother who was studying his thumb which looked like it had been chewed. It had been. And that had happened in a bar fight, I learned later, with a man who had gotten Ernest's hand in his mouth and really leaned into the job of chewing what was available to him.

Ernest was a famous brawler, but this fight had gone against him, and he had come to our house drunk and wounded in the middle of the night because my mother's skill as a former nursing student drew him. I don't know how competent Dorothy Duff really was as a first-aid practitioner, but like all the characteristics reputed to belong to members of the Duff family, her reputation was mythic. Anything possessed by anybody named Duff or connected to the Duffs took on proportions of importance and merit beyond that of what other mortals might claim. All the Duffs said it did, particularly my father, so it had to be true.

We were all conditioned to *believe* the lies we told about ourselves to each other and to anybody else who'd listen, and believing those lies made them true. It had to be that way. All we really owned and claimed was not material. Others had *stuff*. The Duffs had *stories* about stuff.

Ernest was weeping at full bay, my mother was trying to stop the bleeding and figure out whether her cousin by marriage simply had to go to a doctor or if he could get away without doing so, and my father was asking a series of questions designed to wring every detail of the event out of Ernest. I was scared, horrified, tingling all over, and fascinated by what was before me and what had led to all that blood and bone visible in our living room in the middle of the night. No one would pay any attention to me, no matter how loud I cried and pulled at my mother and father, and I couldn't make them realize I believed I was the real victim here, the one most wounded and in need of first aid.

No one listened, though, and it was finally decided that Ernest shouldn't go to the doctor but depend instead on the antiseptic my mother poured over his thumb and the gauze bandage she wrapped around it.

"Go to the doctor, Ernest," she said. "You've got to do it tomorrow. He's going to need to sew it up."

"I can't, Dorothy," Ernest said. "I used brass knucks on the son of a bitch, and they'll stick you in the pen for that in Texas."

"What are brass knucks?" I asked, pulling at my mother's nightgown and knowing what Ernest had just said was the most interesting element that had popped up so far from the bloody scene before me. "Tell me what brass knucks are."

"Shut up, Gerald," my father said. "When did you use them, Ernest? Before he bit you?"

"No, hell, Willie," Ernest said between yowls. "If I'd got to do that, he wouldn't have had the chance to bite me nor nothing else."

"What are brass knucks?" I said. "Tell me about the brass knucks."

"Here," my grown, bloody, and bitten cousin said, reaching with his unchewed hand into his pocket. "Here's the brass knucks. Run hide them in a dresser drawer, Gerald, or a chifforobe."

"No, he won't," my mother said, taking whatever it was Ernest was holding toward me. "I'll take care of this. Willie, take Gerald back to his bed."

"No," I screamed, risking physical punishment myself, "Ernest wants me to do it. I can hide the brass knucks all by myself."

I wasn't allowed to do that, of course, but I found the brass knucks the next day in less than a few minutes rummaging through all the drawers and cabinets and hidey holes used by my mother to keep things from me.

The knucks were impressive, silver-colored and molded with openings to fit over a man's fist for protection and clout, and I used them to slug pillows and walls until I was found out and warned off from ever touching them again. They vanished after that for several weeks, and I didn't run across them again until by accident one day when I was searching for the stash of bubble gum my mother had bought to dole out to me and Nancy one chew and one day at a time.

This instrument was what got a man sent to prison in Texas, I considered as I imagined ways to put them to good use against people like Kenwood Delcambre and the boy who had scratched my back until it bled, years before. Ernest Duff had said brass knucks were that serious, and I was eager to believe him, and proud that they were in the possession of my family. Mess with the Duffs and you're liable to get hit with a fist covered with knucks. See how you like that, then, I would tell myself, my hand snugged into the instrument of mayhem as seriously as I could force it, my head filled with images of boys quailing before me.

One other scene of grown men crying and covered with blood from that time in Nederland helped fill my nightly dreams and contribute to what my mother called my nervousness. It involved Dolly Roberts, but the feelings it gave me had nothing to do with my formless thoughts her legs evoked while I lay on the bed beside her as she read her magazine.

Instead of coming in the middle of the night, this event took place one day near suppertime. I remember that when the action kicked off I was standing by my mother's side as she was frying a piece of meat in an iron skillet. I was hungry enough to want to be close to what my mother was doing, despite having to chance the random danger of grease popping on me out of the pan, when Dolly Roberts came running into the kitchen through the back door to the house, wailing loud, something about her husband, J.D.

"I've got all the knives in the house hid, Dorothy," she said between sobs and outcries, "but I'm afraid he might find them. I didn't have time to hide them real good."

"Why's he looking for knives, Dolly?" my mother said, slamming a lid on the pan of meat and grease and pushing me away from the range. "What's wrong with J.D.?"

"He got in a fight drinking beer at the Model Café with somebody, and he just got beat up all to pieces. He came home looking for a knife to go back and cut the man who did it."

"Can't you get him to go to bed? Willie's not home from work yet or he'd go over there to talk to J.D. How bad hurt is he?"

"He won't lie down, and he keeps opening all the drawers looking and looking and looking for something sharp. He says he's going to come over here to your house and get a knife. He keeps crying and saying, 'I know Dorothy's got a kitchen full of butcher knives, and I'm going to get the biggest one I can lay my hands on.'"

Hearing that instantly made me want to do two things: pee, and simultaneously run next door to watch J.D. look for knives. So I stood there next to the pan full of meat almost done enough to eat, jumping up and down and demanding more details about who had beaten up J.D., and what exactly that beating had done to him.

"Is he bleeding?" I asked Dolly. "Did the man bite him? Did he knock any of J.D.'s teeth out of his mouth? I got to go pee-pee right now."

"Be quiet, Gerald," my mother said. "Go pee-pee and play with your plastic soldiers, and leave Dolly alone."

So I did that, not able to learn anything else about J.D.'s fight in the Model Café until my father got home from Sun Oil and heard the details from my mother. She had spent the time between leaving the supper turned off on the stove and my father's arrival home in Dolly's and J.D.'s house by putting iodine on J.D.'s cuts and bruises and telling him he couldn't go back down to the café to get his revenge.

"He'll be gone by the time you'd get there anyway, J.D.," she told him. "So it'd be a wasted trip."

"I don't even know the son of a bitch's name," J.D. said. "They called him something like Sarge. He's old as the hills, too, the way he looks."

"J.D. doesn't know how to fight," Dolly said to my mother. "He ain't old enough yet for that."

"The shit I don't," J.D. said. "He caught me looking off and just dough-popped me that first lick."

"See what I'm telling you," my mother said. "I told you he'd be gone by the time you got back to kill him. He's scared to death of you."

"You reckon?" J.D. said, tilting his head back to receive medical attention more readily, mollified.

I wasn't present in the Roberts's bedroom to hear this exchange, but I overheard its report by my mother to my father over the warmed-up supper, and the words stuck in my mind well enough for me to repeat them to my sister Nancy over and over for the next several days.

"Then," I told her. "We could hear Dolly hollering and carrying on after it got dark that night. Mama and Daddy told me not to think about it no more and just go to sleep."

"I heard Dolly hollering, too," Nancy said, "all the way over here in our house. I know all about that. You don't have to tell me that part."

I told her anyway, explaining why Dolly was hollering at J.D. in their bedroom, saying it was because she was still worried he'd find a knife and go back down to the Model Café to get even, but I knew that something was going on that didn't explain all of it, something serious enough my parents didn't want me talking about it later. It had to do with how J.D. had been beaten up by an old man named Sarge. All right, I understood and accepted, but I knew that the way Dolly's legs looked when she was lying on her bed with her shoes off had something to do with her outcries as well. What exactly, I didn't know, but it made the same feeling come up in my belly her naked legs did when Dolly kept me in her house while my mother was safely gone somewhere else. I liked the way it made me feel, but I knew I couldn't tell anybody about that, especially my mother.

CHAPTER 7

What Reading Smelled Like

I WAS SITTING IN THE PORCH SWING, MAKING IT MOVE FROM SIDE TO SIDE, SINCE I couldn't reach the floor yet with my feet. I had just learned from my mother that since my birthday came a week after Nederland Elementary School was scheduled to start, I had to wait another whole year before I'd be able to begin the first grade. I didn't know why exactly, but I was happy about the news. I wouldn't have to start learning to read and do number tricks and deal with other people my exact age for another complete year, and that was a great comfort to me. I could stay at home, do such things as make the porch swing move from side to side until it ran with a bang into the house on one side and the banister on the other, pretending I was a character I called "Rackon," a fighter pilot and killer of Germans and Japanese. All the while listening to the radio play the songs my mother liked and the stories about women she paid close attention to, with names like Backstage Wife and Stella Dallas, and I wouldn't have to do what another woman told me to for another whole year.

I had never been to school before, not even kindergarten, since that educational concept was not known in Nederland, Texas, at the time, but I had older cousins already in school and who kept me informed about how hard it was and how people bigger and meaner than you would beat you up, and women with names like Miss Anna and Miss Minnie would order you to do whatever came into their minds. And you had to do what they said, or they would snatch you out of your seat and whip you in front of the others of your age group until you had cried enough to satisfy them.

Being at home with my sister Nancy to order about and tell lies to was much preferable to that, I knew in my bones, so the news that I had to wait until I was almost seven before going off to school made me deeply glad. I swung that porch swing that late summer day of 1944 until the wall I was running it into boomed and chipped and the paint got scar marks all over it.

Most people I have known in my life claim to have learned to read by the time they were five years old or so, having been taught by their mothers and fathers to figure out words on the page long before they began formal learning in school. I never had that experience, and I have never regretted it.

I was read to, all right, from the time I was conscious of being alive, mostly by my father, but it was never with the intent to teach me a skill. Big Willie Duff read to me because I was the only audience he happened to have at the time, and I knew he was doing it as confirmation of the experience he was having at the moment, not because he had an educational intent in mind.

"Come over here, Gerald," my father would say, and I would leave whatever I was doing to enter the force field he occupied.

What he read to me were stories from *Argosy*, *Field and Stream*, *Man*, and especially *True Magazine*, since we believed dealt with stuff that had really happened. Men being attacked by tigers and giant snakes. American prisoners of war being tortured by Jap soldiers with huge teeth and Germans in green and black uniforms, wielding clubs and pliers for pulling out teeth and twisting off noses.

To me, reading stories never had anything to do with learning new, educationally interesting, or possibly useful information. Reading involved entering a space defined by smell and heat and the aura of someone sunk into his own head and satisfaction. There were no ulterior motives, ever. *What is happening between me and these words is something good enough to have someone other than me partake of it as I'm doing it.* That's what my father's reading to me said. That, and nothing else.

My father never read anything he thought was fictional. If a story wasn't true, as he saw it, it wasn't worth the time it would take to look at it. Yet one of the books he liked most, I discovered when I was in graduate school, was not true in the way Willie Duff defined the real. The book was titled *Surrey of the Eagle's Nest*, and it was his favorite because it recounted the exploits of one Major Surrey, an officer on Robert E. Lee's staff during the Civil War, in my father's mind an era of heroism, stoicism, courage in the face of defeat, and a refusal to surrender. My father took it for gospel truth, and he recounted to me many of the exploits of Major Surrey as the young officer endured four years of noble persistence in the Army of Northern Virginia, Lee's fabled command.

In fact, I later learned in a course in the American novel that *Surrey of the Eagle's Nest* was one of many romantic novels about the "Recent Unpleasantness" written by John Esten Cooke of Virginia in the late nineteenth century. It was told from first-person point of view, and therefore my father accepted the account as unqualifiedly real and accurate, believing that no one could make up such thrilling and inspiring tales if he hadn't really experienced them. My first impulse on learning that my father's favorite book was fiction was to tell him that. But I didn't, the good son now keeping the parent in the dark as to what was real and what was not. If my father wanted to believe only in the truth to be found in the verifiably real, that was his right, I considered, and who was I to tell him fiction could get at truth more effectively than any number of journalist renderings of events. Willie Duff wouldn't have believed what I told him about Major Surrey for long anyway.

My father wanted to believe a lie because he thought it was the truth, and I had learned to believe lies because I knew they were not the truth. To each his due, and to each his own perception.

But I couldn't read on my own when I entered the first grade at Nederland Elementary School, called "low school" by the other boys and girls in my class in order to distinguish the experience from whatever was to come in later years, in "high school." I looked upon what my first grade teacher Miss Anna Rienstra was doing with the cards she held up to us—imprinted with letters and numbers and combinations of those which made words—as not what my father dealt with in *True Magazine* but as chores to get through so that I could do what I wanted to get to later. It was like learning to use a knife and fork to eat what was on my plate, instead of just grabbing it up by hand.

A person was making me consume what I needed in a way she considered right and proper, as my mother did, but I knew well I could get the same effect by just picking up the meat or potatoes or piece of cake by hand and cramming it into my mouth.

"What's this one?" Miss Anna would say, holding up the letters spelling out *cat* or *dog* or *apple*, expecting and demanding that we sound out the letters, while I wanted to just jump in and call it what it was as quick as I could.

That habit was one of the things that caused me to be so unpopular with my classmates after a short period of time. I always finished the reading and math and coloring assignments given us to perform in class before anybody else did, and then I turned around in my seat (I always sat in the front row when I had a choice until I learned later, much too late to do me any good, to avoid calling attention to myself by such stunts), and I watched the rest of them struggle with what our teacher had told us to do. "Look at Gerald Duff," J.W. Slater said aloud once when I did that, "sitting up there already finished and just a-looking at us." I could tell J.W.'s comment was hate-filled, and that surprised me but also made me glad. His bottom lip was too big and hung down unattractively, I remember, and he ate paste. We all did that, of course, though never as much as he and Joe Stuckey did. Joe Stuckey's name had something to do with his appetite for paste, I sensed, and that helped me learn early the connection between names and the way the right choice of them made sense of what went on in the world.

But when Miss Anna Rienstra made us all call out what we saw on the flash cards she held before us, I eagerly joined in, sometimes so excited by recognizing words I knew I'd be able to find later in stories about Japanese torture methods and hunts for man-eating tigers that I had to reach down and hold the front of my pants to keep from peeing all over myself.

I talked out loud in class, I ate candy from my pockets, I stood up when I was supposed to be sitting, I pulled the pigtails of Reba Williams, I stuck my pencil up the ringlets of red hair cascading from the head of Hilda Robicheaux to see how that would look, and I got my hands spanked with a ruler by Miss Anna for each of these infractions. Once I was kept after school for something I had done, and broke into tears when I had to go home alone with a dark cloud building in the Gulf Coast sky above me. That concerned even Miss Anna who recognized the extent of my hysteria and followed me at a distance until I got into sight of my house with my mother standing on the front porch wondering where I was.

I expect Miss Anna faded into the bushes on the side of the shell-covered road at the sight of the look on Dorothy Duff's face.

But the worst thing that happened to me during the four years of "low school" in Nederland was the day I crapped my pants in class, not nearly close enough to the end of the day to leave, forcing me to sit in an aura of stink that made all my classmates remark bitterly on how bad Gerald smelled. By the time I finally got home, some of the excess had worked its way up the back of my pants and got on my new cowboy belt, permanently leaving a mark which made it unwearable in my mind from that point forward.

My father was not sympathetic, though my mother was, and he made it clear he considered my response to the accident to be one and the same with my incessant fingernail biting and the night terrors which sent me squalling time and time again to his and my mother's bed, complaining about tigers and Japanese with big teeth.

He got his comeuppance shortly after that event, though what he suffered had more effect on me, my sister, and my mother than it ever did on him. When bad things happen to parents, I first learned then, the cost brings much more blood from the offspring than it does from the old folks.

CHAPTER 8

The Fall from Grace

It happened early in my fourth grade, just before Halloween, because I remember having in my hand a sheaf of construction paper cut into the silhouettes of black cats and witches on broomsticks as I arrived home that afternoon from school. My father and mother were standing on the front porch of the house just off Detroit Street in Nederland, my mother was crying, and my father's face was even redder than its ordinary hue, a shade just this side of the red ball on the Japanese flag. The war had been over for several years by then, and bucktoothed Japanese soldiers had ceased to feature so regularly in my nightmares, but the color red still made me uneasy.

Big Willie, all six feet, five inches and 240 pounds of him, had been told that day he was laid off from the employ of the Sun Oil Company. He was forty-eight years old, he had turned down a short time earlier an offer to be made "time-keeper" of his crew, and he had done that because he knew the responsibilities of the post would make him unpopular with the men whose time he would be keeping. Things were slowing down in 19?? economies of scale were kicking in, the burden of salary had to be cut—all these business realities were coming to bear, and the Sun Oil workers were proudly not unionized. They had never before needed to band together for protection, so why should they now? I figured all this out years later, but at the time my father became unemployed as a "hand" in the petro-chemical industry of the Texas Gulf Coast I believed the story he clung to and the one he told my mother and anyone who would listen to him.

He had stood up to some unfair interpretation of work conditions, he had voiced what others of his coworkers, people named Little Willie and Hoodlum Red and Courts and Commalander and Hollywood VanZandt and Dolphus and Tack Hammer, were afraid to say, and they had kept their jobs, but my father had not. He spoke out, and he was sacrificed.

At the time I imagined the event to have been one in which all these men and others, along with my father, Big Willie Duff, were stood up in a line facing the Boss who had a piece of paper in his hand with the names of the winners and losers written on it. He read aloud from it, calling off the list of those allowed to stay on the job and draw their hourly wages and finally saying something like this: "Big Willie, you and Doucette and LeBlanc and Brazile and Moye don't work for the Sun Oil Company no more. Don't come back here again, never."

Then the ones who could still work picked up their tools, and my father and the others cast out from the Sun walked toward the gate to the world outside, bleak and gray and plumb out of paychecks.

He could have found a job somewhere else in the Golden Triangle of Texas. Hiring was continual at that time so soon after the war, but my father couldn't accept the rejection by the Sun Oil Company, a firm headquartered in Philadelphia, Pennsylvania, way off up north, as he frequently told me, so he packed us all up: me, my sister Nancy, and my mother—pregnant at forty-one with her last child who would be Wilma, named for our father—and he took us off to Polk County, Texas, where he had grown up and where no work for "hands" had existed since all the virgin pine and hardwood timber had been logged off to the bare ground during the previous fifty years.

He took the loss of his job at Sun Oil as deeply as Adam must have done when he was expelled from Eden, and Big Willie retreated to Polk County, where liquor was outlawed and Texas's only Indian reservation was located, and Duffs of every description and small-mindedness lived and wandered, watching and critiquing each other's every deed, habit, thought, and predilection.

Willie Duff was home again, and the starving time had begun.

We moved into one side of my Aunt MayBelle's rent-house in Livingston, Texas, the one next door to Aunt Rosalie's house. Aunt MayBelle had never married, and she had lived all her adult life with her big sister in one room of the house Rosalie lived in with her husband Lem. Lemuel Archibald Richardson had his own room in the rear of the house where he stayed when he wasn't lying on the sofa. The two children he had fathered with Rosalie were L.A. and Jewel. L.A. became a ministerial student at East Texas Bible College in Marshall, arguably the worst school in Texas and thus in the entire universe. Jewel was a tall, *plain-featured* girl, as my father called her, and a scholar of note at Livingston High School. She would graduate as valedictorian, beating out her competition Beth Gerlach by one hundredth of a point. Once I saw Jewel's annual from her senior year and read in it Beth Gerlach's inscription to her friendly rival. "To Jewel," Beth had penned in beautifully regular script, "the cheating valedictorian."

I never could figure out why Jewel had let her sworn enemy write in her annual in the first place and after having read what Beth Gerlach had said about her, why she hadn't blotted it out. "Don't you dare say anything to Jewel about it," my mother told me. "If you do, she'll kill you, if I don't do it first."

Our living in Aunt MayBelle's house was part of my father's grand plan to seek vengeance on the Sun Oil Company. We would move from our house in Nederland, rental though it was, with five rooms and a kitchen (no bathroom, though; we used an outhouse on the back edge of the lot, but it was a nice one with a cement throne and a good roof), to two rooms in Aunt MayBelle's house, counting the kitchen where my bed was (no bathroom and a very inferior outhouse full of wasp nests and spider webs and with a wooden throne). My father would not work because he would pose as unable to do so, having injured his back in the employ of the Sun Oil Company, and Big Willie would wait for his legal suit to reach success in a Jefferson County courthouse in Beaumont.

In the meantime, Nancy and I would attend school in Livingston, my mother would find some way to feed us all with no paychecks coming in and to keep us clothed while she waited for her baby to be born, and my father's sisters would resent our presence on a minute-by-minute basis.

The experience in its entirety prepared me to understand to the bone when I first read *King Lear* years later, what Shakespeare was getting at when he had the deposed king say when questioned about his need for retainers, "Reason not the need."

We lived in one side of MayBelle Duff's house cooped up in the second act of my father's own personal Elizabethan drama for over two years. I would think it can't get worse than this, as I stood each morning waiting for the school bus to haul us to Livingston Elementary School, hoping that Bucky Brock and Doug Bell and the others wouldn't pelt me with pine cones in the face this time. On my back was bearable, and on the arms and legs I could stand, but the ones to the face stung like fire.

The court case was settled eventually, and my mother and father announced that fact to the world at large as a triumph and a vindication of Willie Duff's assertions of being wronged by Sun. Truth had won out. Willie Duff had been cheated and mistreated and left for dead on the side of the road. See, the courts of Jefferson County had said so. So look on that, you mighty, and despair.

The total amount of payout was a little over $4,000, but the lawyer got a large share, and my father had to pay Aunt MayBelle the accrued rent for the two years in her house, enough so that when the check was securely in my parents' possession, there wasn't enough to allow them to buy me and Nancy bicycles after all. I got a plastic slingshot, I think, and Nancy got a doll that would wet.

But the redeeming feature of that time in Aunt MayBelle's rent house was that I learned to lie expertly and convincingly. I had already shown a talent for making things up, but the two-year hitch in two rooms of Aunt MayBelle's place perfected it.

It was Christmas time in East Texas, especially in Miss Amerine's fourth-grade class, and all the decorations were up on the walls and door facings. I had responded to the teacher's challenge that we all draw a picture of either Baby Jesus, or the entire manger scene including reverent barnyard animals and visiting kings, or some other representation of our own devising, and I had done so by imagining a worshipful turkey which had shown up to recognize the birth of the Messiah.

My attempts at a more encompassing emblem had come to naught, so I decided a recycling of a turkey I had done in honor of Thanksgiving the previous month would do. I knew how to draw around my spread fingers and thumb already, and I figured I would take advantage of that skill by adding a halo to the turkey's head and pouring in an especially heavy layer of Crayola brown, red, and gold.

Miss Amerine had told us she would pin each of our creations to a string she had tied across the top of the blackboard, and she would do so in the order of the quality of accomplishment by each Livingston fourth-grader. When we all arrived the morning after the day we had presented our work to the teacher, the display was up, and I immediately looked at the position of honor, the first one, found Linda Lee Smith's drawing there, not my Christ-adoring turkey, and began working my way down the order. Mine was last, I discovered, easy to pick out of all the others because of the sheen of brown wax I had loaded into my piece and then attempted to scrape off with a protractor, a layer I had decided was overkill. Instinctively, I had realized it reeked too much of late Van Gogh, though I didn't know of that artist's work at the time.

That critical judgment by my teacher rocked me, accustomed as I was to being first in all things scholastic though last in the social structure of Miss Amerine's classroom, and I was much cast down. I still feel it today.

My perfection in lying did spring from the wreckage of that artistic disaster, however, and a birth took place.

CHAPTER 9

A Talent for the Lie

When we came back to school after the holiday for Christmas, Miss Amerine had each of us stand up in front of the room and tell our classmates what Santa Claus had brought us on the birthday of Jesus. Here I saw my chance to reestablish my rightful position as first and foremost, and I did. I hadn't been given a chance to plan my remarks, but the pressure of the moment inspired me to outdo myself in originality and force.

I began with the big one, the new bicycle, the Schwinn with all accessories including the horn in the console, moved to the red wagon with wooden side extensions, the Red Ryder air rifle, segued to the cap pistols (a matched pair), the pup tent which had been used in the war against the Japanese (complete with patched bullet holes from an attack which had been successfully foiled but not before gouts of blood stained the canvas), and was warming to a description of the pony, which abruptly ended when Miss Amerine broke in and made me sit down.

"That's enough, Gerald," she told me. "Let somebody else have a chance to talk."

I sat down, halted in mid-career, but not downcast by that fact. I figured it would take a heroic effort from any one of my classmates to match what I had been allowed to register in public as my Christmas gifts, and I knew that not a one of them could make up as many lies as I had just done on the spur of the moment, not if they had a week to prepare, bound as they all were to the literal.

When I got home that afternoon, I told my mother of my triumph, speaking so fast and stuttering so much she made me sit down to finish. I was surprised by her response, since what she said was that I had overdone it in describing all the gifts I had received from Santa Claus.

"You know there is no Santa Claus, don't you, Gerald?" she said. "That's just a story for little boys and girls, like Nancy and Wilma, and you're old enough to know better than that."

I blustered my way through assuring her I did know the truth of the lie she and my father had been perpetuating for years, and of course I did know there was no kindly man who traveled about the world one day a year giving out presents to people like me. But I had never let myself think about that fact, and I did know I hadn't received even one of the things I bragged about to my fourth-grade classmates, and I knew in my bones that while I was telling the lie I believed it myself. And it made me feel good while doing it.

I could see the Schwinn bicycle I never received, and I could smell the pony in the backyard eating the weeds that grew there. I did then and I still can now, whenever I want to, and sometimes at night waiting for sleep, I let that happen.

The fact that my parents had been lying to me for years about the existence of such a myth didn't bother me. They had lied to me about other matters before, in particular to me and Nancy about the birth of our little sister Wilma, the coming of whom I knew nothing about until I arrived home from school one day to find my mother and father absent and Aunt MayBelle waiting to tell me and Nancy where they were.

"They have gone to the hospital to get a baby that nobody else wanted, you see," she said, "and they'll be home with her tomorrow."

"What is it?" I said.

"It's a girl named Wilma."

"I don't like that name," I said.

"Why did they want to get a baby nobody else wanted?" Nancy asked. "We don't need a baby around here. Tell them to leave it there at the hospital."

Years later, on my first reading of Thomas Hardy's *Jude the Obscure*, I knew precisely why Little Father Time had hanged himself upon learning of the birth of another child to Sue Bridehead. Like my sister Nancy, he thought the coming of the new child was made by choice, and he understood his parents were fools to get another one when they had any other option to pursue.

That's one reason Nancy and I have never been close to Wilma since that moment we were told that our foolish mother and father, in the face of living in two rooms with the toilet outside, with no paycheck coming in, with the typical meal for us being biscuits and flour gravy and fried fatback and huge butterbeans, had hied themselves to downtown Livingston, Texas, to pick up a baby nobody else wanted. Nancy and I sure didn't want her, either.

That's one reason we aren't close to her. The other reason we seldom see or communicate with Wilma, who renamed herself Janice when she was fourteen years old and has never smiled spontaneously at either of her siblings for a lifetime, is that she has worked at and proved to be over the years like all youngest siblings, last come and first served.

CHAPTER 10

The Water We Had to Drink

Soon after Willie Duff received his court settlement from the Sun Oil Company, he moved us out of his sister's renthouse into the country, fifteen miles from Livingston, and us with no car. There was no family automobile until I bought a 1952 Dodge sedan for $300 when I was a freshman at Lamar State College of Technology. He installed us in a tiny house rented for six dollars a month from Carl Vinson. When we left that house several years later, my father had not been able to pay the rent for eighteen months, so we left without saying goodbye to Carl, owing him over a hundred dollars back rent.

The house in the country was located across the road, Texas Farm to Market Highway 1276, from a country store operated by Estol Collins. The only Indian reservation in Texas, home to the Alabama-Coushatta Nation, was down the highway a few miles. In the other direction was the sawmill community of Camp Ruby, abandoned by all but a handful of families after the Carter Lumber Company finished cutting all the timber in that part of the Piney Woods and vanished. What was left were fallen-down houses, huge piles of sawdust in which weeds and briars and saplings grew, the company commissary store, Camp Ruby Baptist Church, and a collection of residents too weak, unmotivated, ambitionless, played-out, slow-witted, and lacking in imagination to follow the company's lead and get the hell out.

Our house had three rooms. The first one you entered was the living area, complete with a woodstove connected to a pipe running through the roof. To the right was a bedroom where my parents slept, and through a door to the rear was the third room, a combined kitchen with a table for meals, another woodstove for cooking, and a bed in the corner where I slept along with my sister until we both got so old we rebelled against sharing a mattress. At that point Nancy moved all her sleeping to a sofa in the living room.

A little shelf was attached to the wall by the back door, and on it were a bucket, a tin dipper, and a wash basin. That was the plumbing. Outdoors to the right was a bored well, as opposed to what was called a dug well. Bored was upscale and high-tech in the context of East Texas country living and marked a property as much more desirable than one with water provided by a dug well. I remember my father explaining its merits to me in detail.

"The main thing, Gerald," he said, "is you can cover up a bored well with something to keep stuff from falling in. You can't do that with a dug well."

"What kind of stuff?"

"Trash. Squirrels, birds, cats, dirt," he said. "Stuff like that. Another thing, see, is that bored wells are a lot deeper than dug wells, because, you see, they're bored. Not dug."

"A machine did it," I said to my father.

"Yeah. That's right, and that machine boring so deep will put you into a purer water table. You'll get right down into a stream of water, a river maybe, underneath the ground. With a dug well, you get a whole lot of run-off and rain water. Gets all muddied up."

That was a comfort to a degree, except that the water from our bored well did get muddied up from heavy rains, giving it an off-yellow color. It also contained some species of small many-legged insects resembling shrimp which had to be strained out through a mesh filter, and the water from it had to be pulled up by hand in a thin metal container attached to a rope which ran through a pulley. I was the main drawer of water and hewer of wood for the Willie Duff family enterprise, and I must have pulled up thousands of gallons of water during the years we lived in Carl Vinson's rent house.

I didn't mind the water-drawing, for the most part, except on Saturdays when I had to fill tubs of it for the rinsing of the clothes my mother and my sister washed in the machine kept on the front porch. It was a wringer-washer, which meant you had to watch your fingers when running wet clothes through the rollers.

Apart from dreading the sight of the shrimp bugs as I strained them through the mesh for each bucket of water we used for drinking and cooking, I wasn't overly repelled by this chore. The frequency and number of the living creatures we had to strain out depended on factors which were a puzzle. Sometimes there were more of them, sometimes less, but one thing was certain. We never told anyone outside the family about their existence, and that was another of the lies I learned to maintain in order to allow us to go on pretending we weren't that different from other people in our part of East Texas. Why we were plagued with foreign life in our water supply was unanswerable, like many other aspects of our living conditions, but all of us knew it was something to hide, it was shameful, and it was somehow our fault. The earth gave us nasty stuff to strain out before we could use the necessity it provided, so we kept our mouths shut and did what we had to do to survive.

One day in particular of my water-drawing from our bored well stands out in memory, enough so that I've dreamed about it over the years on a frequent basis, typically when something has gone less than satisfactorily in my day. Say an argument with one of my wives, or a humiliation at work, or a rejection by some editor or agent or reviewer of something I've written. Then the squirming, tiny, many-legged, almost transparent beasts at home in what I've got to swallow to be able to live will come floating up, and I've got no choice but to strain them out and drink down the stuff they come from.

That day my mother was at the well drawing a bucket of water. She had probably decided it was easier to do it herself rather than get me to stop reading whatever book I was sunk into, and she had gone outside to do the job. I heard Nancy screaming, and I ran outside to see why. Was there a snake? Or a stray hog, a piney woods rooter as they were called, that had wandered up? Had our sister Wilma hurt herself? Or was Nancy just acting crazy again?

I saw Nancy standing beside our mother who was lying on the ground unconscious, the well bucket beside her with its rope strung across her upper body and the bucket the water was to be poured into overturned beside her.

"Mama's dead," Nancy said. "She just fell over and her eyes rolled back in her head and all you can see's the whites of them."

She wasn't dead, just anemic and rundown and probably suffering from the early effects of the cancer that would kill her a few years later, and after I had drawn another bucket of water and let it gush over her face, she roused. What happened next I don't recall, but I remember the terror I felt realizing that my mother could, in fact, die. What would come of us then? With her gone and Willie Ellis Duff in full charge of the family, I knew in my bones we'd be doomed.

Thoughts of impending doom loomed large after we had moved from Livingston out into the country near Camp Ruby. Everything around us spoke of that—my father's intermittent employment as a logger, as a brush cutter for various pipeline companies pushing through another link for oil and gas for states north of Texas, as a trimmer of pine logs for telephone poles, as a cotton picker on his nephew's farm—all endeavors which brought in money now and then, but never enough to buy what we needed. Doom and fear buzzed in the air, day and night. For the first time in my life we began to attend church.

CHAPTER 11

Washed in the Blood

AT LEAST, MY MOTHER AND MY SISTERS AND I BEGAN GOING TO CHURCH, NEVER my father, who at that point in his life still had a bellyful of what he had been raised doing as a son and a grandson of Baptist preachers. His father Amos and his grandfather James had both been famous as backwoods Baptist ministers, and Willie had suffered through that upbringing from birth until he made his break for the Gulf Coast. Not until he was confined in a nursing home years later did my father rediscover a need to get right with Jesus.

So while my mother and sisters and I went every Sunday morning and Sunday night and Wednesday night to the Camp Ruby Baptist Church, he stayed home if he was not out looking for work. My family hadn't needed churchgoing when we lived in Nederland, and we hadn't gone to church in Livingston where we didn't have the clothes for it, but in the Camp Ruby community, we joined the rest of the hopeless and rump-sprung inhabitants in worship services every time the door opened.

For my mother, the Camp Ruby Baptist Church offered somewhere to go, a place where she could talk to other people, an outlet for her ability to play the piano, and maybe a connection with a higher power that could bring her family some groceries, clothes, furniture, and a way out of the situation we were in.

Being raised in a family descended from nineteenth-century immigrants from Ireland, Dorothy Jane Irwin had always been superstitious, and now religion was worth a try, though I'm certain she never thought of her leading us to regular worship of the Southern Baptist god in those terms. Luck and the lack of it were real, opening an umbrella in the house was a terrible and stupid thing to do, drinking milk while eating fish was fatal, breaking a mirror was a seven-year sentence to ill fortune, and probably God was real, too, except He didn't listen very well or seem to give a damn about the situation of the Duff family.

But we kept Him advised about what was going on and what we needed and wanted, so He had no excuse to say He wasn't being kept current. "Pray your daddy gets a job," my mother would say, on the occasions when the advisability arose of reminding the Deity that a nice little shove would be helpful and much appreciated. Maybe Brown and Root would be putting a new pipeline through from Houston to Oklahoma City, and God would be willing to arrange employment on the right-of-way crew for Willie Duff, if we children asked Him nicely. Maybe He would respond quicker and more fully to the pleas of a child than He had proved willing so far to do when grown people came whining and trying to cut a deal with Him.

It was worth a try certainly, prayer and churchgoing, so we caught rides with fellow seekers each day of the week the Camp Ruby church was open, and we showed up. I did my reading assignments for Sunday school and Training Union and Prayer Meeting, and I excelled in Sword Drill, which was the name given to the race to be the first to find a verse thrown out as jump ball by our religious instructors. I knew the answers to the questions about the meaning of Scripture and the connections between one character and another in the Old and New Testaments. I could do biblical exegesis with the best of the locals, though I didn't know I was doing it.

And, as usual, my being first in such endeavors cost me dearly with my peers. Not one of the males near my age in the Camp Ruby Baptist Church could abide being around me, and I didn't blame them. Nothing I knew about or cared about or did or could do connected in any way with those people. For one thing, all of them went to school at Big Sandy, a country institution of only a couple of hundred or so students in all twelve grades. Their fathers were farmers or unemployed sawmill workers or people who had never worked a day. They had last names like Tolar, Brazile, Moy, Pickens, Dikes, Dillon, and Redd. About half the school was made up of Alabama-Coushatta Indian youth, and they were as misplaced as I was. The white students of Big Sandy liked hillbilly music, in a time when it was called that because that's what it was, hillbilly music, and to my ears was a collection of high-pitched groans, whines, and foot-stomps. No one knew or cared what the Indians liked. There were no blacks within twenty miles, and the birth of rock and roll came to me completely over the radio.

The church-goers of my age squatted on their hindquarters in the yard of the church before services began, spitting into doodle bug holes to confuse the inhabitants. They told jokes like, "What did the skirt say?" To which the answer was, "Love lifted me," that phrase a verse from a hymn often sung in Camp Ruby Baptist Church. No one in the bunch ever initiated a conversation with me.

Once in Sunday school, I heard Barney Lee Richards talking to Eblina Lopez, one of the female children of the only Mexican family left in Camp Ruby after the Carter Lumber Company closed the sawmill and left. Eblina was several years older than I, as was Barney Lee Richards, and she was quite smitten with him. He was white, he played basketball on the Big Sandy Wildcats team, and he drove around in his father's old Ford coupe.

"Eblina," Barney Lee said during the exchange, "if I was to ask you if I could do something, would you let me do it?"

"Yeah," Eblina said, and all of us younger Sunday school worshippers instantly knew what the two of them were talking about, though they never said the word itself.

"Can I stick it in?" Barney Lee said.

"If you'll pull it out again, you can," Eblina said in what I took to be a sultry and commanding tone. "But you'll have to put it back in again."

"How many times can I do it?" Barney Lee said, looking around at all of us to be sure we were listening. We were, since this exchange was considered highly coded badinage where we lived. Later that morning, in fact, Larry Wayne Overstreet and I argued about whether Eblina and Barney Lee were or were not talking about "doing it." Larry Wayne didn't think so, and I couldn't convince him otherwise.

"If you move it, I'll groove it," Eblina said, and then Mr. Collins called us all to order to discuss the story of Zacchaeus, the wee little man who climbed up into a sycamore tree his Jesus for to see. That was from another hymn.

Camp Ruby Baptist Church services were, for the young, an arousing break in the tedium of the week, not only for the sexual aristocrats like Eblina Lopez and Barney Lee Richards, but even for someone like me, the weird skinny boy who knew all the answers in the Bible quizzes. I learned one night that if I slumped in my pew and shoved my foot up against that of Betty Overstreet who sat in front that she'd play footsie even with me.

We did that for at least two years, during most services, and I looked forward to our sessions each time I went to church. Nothing more than that ever happened between me and Betty, and I never expected nor wanted more contact than that with Betty, a big red-haired decidedly plain girl one of whose brothers was scarily retarded. But I rubbed up against Betty's feet as long as she'd let me, not only because it was a relief from having to listen to the sermons being delivered by a series of earnest fools in the pulpit, but because of the way Betty's foot action made my groin feel.

I tried the same thing once with Beulahdene Dillon, but she just moved her feet out of range and Betty knew what I was up to, so she withdrew her foot favors for a couple of church services before letting me resume. Betty was a jealous footsie player, and I learned something about women from her response to my attempted dalliance with a strange female.

But going to Camp Ruby Baptist Church wasn't all sexual action, even of the limited sort I enjoyed. Most of it was listening to preachers old and young, slick and fuzzy, unlettered and in seminary, rant against the Roman Catholic Church of which there was not one within fifty miles, and in particular remind me constantly of my sinfulness and the hellfire sure to singe me forever if I didn't accept Jesus Christ as my personal savior.

To do that required a public acknowledgment of the decision to do so, which meant leaving my seat and walking up the aisle during the hymn of invitation, taking the hand of the preacher who stood waiting to receive sinners, and letting people slobber and cry over another lost sinner come to Jesus. The upside of the deal was that all sins were forgiven forever. Once I was saved from Satan's power I'd be saved forever.

It came to me almost instantly upon hearing that truth announced that I'd be fireproof no matter what I would happen to do in the future after I had made the deal with the Deity. I could kill people, I could jack off to my heart's content, I could steal, rob, talk back to adults, drink whiskey and smoke cigarettes, and all Jesus and his father God could do about it was regret the contract They had offered to such a deceptive and low-life bastard as me.

It wasn't until I was in college in a western civilization course that I heard my theological response had a name, antinomianism, a long history of debate in Calvinist theology, and deep roots in Scottish ways of thinking. All I came to know at the time in Camp Ruby was that if I could steel myself to take that humiliating and disheartening walk up the aisle I'd be free of sin, free from the pressure of adults around me urging me to accept Jesus as my savior, and that later on I could have fun anyway. In a graduate seminar in prose fiction at the University of Illinois years later, I read James Hogg's early nineteenth-century novel, *The Private Memoirs and Confessions of a Justified Sinner*, and true enlightenment and historical resonance settled in my mind like stone.

So one night I decided to do it. I was fourteen years old, (well past the age when God might have given me a free pass, which was around twelve at that point if He was in a good mood, and who could predict that?), and I was sick of people to whom I was not even kin sidling up to me during the invitation hymn to urge me to take that first step.

I remember some old woman, maybe Mrs. Dolph Collins, having spoken to me the Sunday before during the last verse of "Just as I Am" in explanation of the process of going up the aisle.

"Son," she said, breathing her old lady smell of powder and light sweat into my face, "all you got to do is take that first step. The rest of them Jesus will take for you, but that first one has got to be yours by yourself."

I held my breath and pretended not to hear, but I could see my mother at the piano near the altar coaxing another few notes of "Just as I Am" out of the instrument which had last been tuned in the Coolidge administration. She was watching the exchange between me and Mrs. Collins, and she was outraged, of course, and that gave me the strength to continue in my hardhearted ignoring of the old fool beside me.

But the time was near, I knew, when my mother would speak to me herself about my soul's salvation, and *that* I couldn't have borne. Besides, my cousin L.A. Richardson was preaching the night Mrs. Collins put the move on me, and to accept Jesus as my personal savior as a result of being shepherded to salvation by him would have been deeply humiliating. I didn't know exactly why it would have been so shameful to have been led to ultimate safety in Gloryland by my first cousin, but I sensed in my bones that giving over sovereignty of myself to someone like L.A. and what he represented—the Duff family writ large—would have been a form of self-betrayal amounting to suicide.

I would be damned to hell before I let L.A. and his mother, Aunt Rosalie, put my scalp on his belt.

So I resisted that night, putting off my surrender until later and in the process—as had been explained by numerous Baptist preachers in their attempts to close the deal during the invitation hymn—left my soul in mortal danger.

"What might happen tonight after you've said 'No, Lord, I'll wait until next week or next month or until a more convenient time to say yes to Jesus?'" the preachers would say, pausing dramatically to look around the congregation, attempting to catch the eyes of known sinners, confirmed in postponement and spiritual laziness. "I'll tell you what might happen. You might leave this place of worship, get into the vehicle which will take you to your home, and in the journey to your place of abode, be involved in an automobile accident which takes your mortal life. Where will you be then, O lost sinner? At the gates of pearl and rosewood and alabaster, you'll stand for the only time in eternity that you'll be allowed to look through the fence into paradise. And you'll say, 'O Lord, I was meaning to accept Jesus Christ as my personal savior next' week. And now this accident has occurred, and can't You just this once allow me to enter paradise to dwell with the saints forever?' And the Lord will say, 'No, I'm sorry, My heart is broken, but you've had the chance each man, each woman, each child is granted, and you've missed the opportunity through sloth and indolence and hardheartedness. So long and goodbye, my child. You've got an appointment elsewhere, and your escort is waiting to lead you into the fire eternal.'"

Slavering behind the lost, postponing, sorry bastard of a sinner would be, if not Satan himself, one of his nasty-handed demons, pitchfork at the ready and the gleam of hellfire in his narrow pig-like eyes. That was a situation to be considered.

Lucky for me, that night my cousin L.A., professionally good in every important sense, had been unable to make the drive to Camp Ruby from East Texas Bible College in Marshall, and had traded off an appearance with a fellow seminarian, one Brother Bill Tate.

As soon as I saw him enter the building and take the pulpit, I knew my chance at being "once saved, always saved" was at hand. If I could muster up the courage to take that first step and let Jesus take the rest of them, I could make a public declaration of my decision to accept the Prince of Peace as my personal savior and not have it all be owed to L.A. Richardson and his mother, my Aunt Rosalie.

Besides, Brother Bill Tate was a lot more interesting-looking than L.A. By the way the women and girls responded to him, they all thought so, too, and the previous week L.A., in announcing the deal he had worked to get a preacher to substitute for him, had said that Brother Bill Tate was a football player at Eaty Becy, as the college was popularly called, he was a jokester, and he even had a nickname, an accomplishment L.A. was never to acquire. Nor me, for that matter. The nickname of L.A.'s fellow Baptist seminarian was Tater Bill, and the romance of that handle fascinated me. To be a Christian saved by grace and willing to talk about it publicly and yet be a college football player called Tater Bill—this combination seemed to be one I would be able to live with.

So as soon as Brother Tater Bill began to preach that night of my fourteenth year in the world (at least two years beyond the point where hair began to grow on my body in new places and where God might take it easier on me if I died right then), I began to get myself ready to take that first step, the one I had to do myself, but the only one, as all had assured me, and make a public declaration of my acceptance of Jesus Christ as my personal savior there in the Camp Ruby Baptist Church. It would be done, it would be over with, I would be saved now and forever, no matter what kind of stunt I might pull in the future, and there wasn't a thing God could do to go back on His word. He wrote the contract; all I would be doing was signing it.

I don't remember the text of Tater Bill's sermon that night of my salvation. I was too busy steeling myself for the humiliation ahead to listen to what slant he was taking, but I do recall that at the end of his sermon the hymn of invitation my mother played on the tuneless piano of the Camp Ruby church was "Softly and Tenderly," a real tearjerker. "Softly and tenderly, Jesus is calling," the nineteenth-century fanatic who wrote the piece had penned in some lonely room, "calling to you and to me. Come home, come home, ye who are weary come home." So by the time the second verse was sung by the collection of thirty or forty worshippers—it was a Sunday night service, the real preacher wasn't there (praise Jesus!), and only the older widows and a few of the horny young were present—I slung my Broadman hymnal to the pew and took that first step on my own, hopeful that Jesus would do the rest of them for me as I had been promised by numerous old ladies and sweaty preachers. He didn't do it, though, and I discovered that the second step, and the third, and all the rest were just as hard for me to do as that first one had been.

Once started, I didn't turn around, though, manfully sticking to the job until I arrived before Brother Bill Tate, onetime college football player, though not at a real college, of course, only Eaty Becy, and he stood dumbfounded as I offered him my hand. Tater Bill's astonishment was clear. I expect he had never saved a soul from the fires of hell on a visiting gig before, expecting only to get his twenty dollars and gas money before he turned around to drive back to Marshall, Texas, and the dormitory bed waiting for him.

But here it was, he had saved his college buddy's cousin from the snares of Satan without even trying to do it, and all the congregation was focused on the drama being enacted before them. With great presence of mind, Tater Bill forced me to my knees to pray beside him, and I sank to the floor, desperate for Jesus to come on through and uphold His part of the deal. I had been told after the first step the Savior would come on in there and give me a hand, and I was counting on that to get me through the shame and embarrassment of the public statement I was making.

He didn't, though. I didn't feel one bit of spiritual uplift or exaltation as I kneeled in surrender, and I realized the whole promise of divine help to come after I had made the first gesture was just another lie from the adults that surrounded me. It wasn't a conscious lie, I knew, since they probably believed what they were saying, all being capable of massive self-deception, and it could have been true that Jesus did help them in their own declaration of the acceptance of Him as personal savior. The Lamb of God was possibly withholding help from me out of spite and personal animus. He didn't really like me, much less love me divinely, and He was deriving satisfaction from my discomfort and public shame.

After the prayer there on the splintery floor of the church, the shiny nailheads holding it all together now the focus of my attention as Tater Bill asked for and got abject confession of surrender from me ("Gerald, do you know what you're doing? Do you understand the commitment you now owe to God and His son, Jesus Christ? Can't you feel His love welling up in your heart as we kneel here together? Do you realize the rejoicing among the angels that's going on at this minute in Heaven?" My response to all these queries: "Yessir, yessir, yessir."), I was allowed to rise, turn, and face the congregation. They came forward one by one, the old ladies whose kisses on my face felt like lukewarm worms crawling, the odd old man or two clapping me on the shoulder and pumping my hand in their palms hardened by work in truck gardens and logging woods and under the hoods of pickups and failing sedans, the slow-footed members of the Eck Overstreet family (male and female, old and young, drooling and dry-faced), and the worst of all, the ones my age, witness now to my comeuppance.

They knew what was happening, the young ones. I was brought down, not so smart now, just another one gone over to dwell with the saints forever, no longer the holdout, but simply another fool who in public declaration had taken Jesus Christ as personal savior and admitted I'm just like you are, after all. What comes to mind now is the inscription below the death date on the gravestone of my great-grandfather James Edward Duff, buried in the Big Sandy cemetery. "Just another sinner saved by grace," it declares, an announcement of selfhood consumed by ordinariness and kinship. I'm no different from the herd, my great-grandfather's statement admits. Hell, no matter how I've held myself up before you until now, I'm just the same as you.

That's what I felt as I left the church afterwards and crawled into the bed of Maggie Lee Overstreet's pickup that would ferry me and my family the three miles home. I'm like the rest of them now. I've admitted it to the whole damn bunch, and now maybe they'll let me alone. At least, I'll be saved from hell and now able to spend eternity in Heaven skipping down streets of gold completely at peace. Tell yourself that, Gerald, I said inside my head. It'll make up for what you had to do tonight on the floor of the Camp Ruby Baptist Church.

But when my sister Nancy, riding in the pickup bed beside me in the dark, asked how I felt now—"Is it different to be a Christian? Do you feel born again, like L.A. and the rest of them are always saying? Are you a different person?"—I knew in my newly converted soul that nothing had changed. I'd still want to play footsie with girls, look at pictures of naked grown women, listen to colored people sing rock and roll on the radio, get my own way on each and every occasion that arose, and be the same selfish boy I'd always been. Looking up at the dead stars above the pickup, so impossibly far away, I wished for some different feeling to kick in just below my breastbone, that place that always felt so tight and twisted when I was under duress. But it didn't kick in, want it though I did, all the way home in the bed of Maggie Lee Overstreet's pickup, it didn't kick in the next morning when the sun came up and everybody stepped around me awkwardly with averted eyes, and it never has, to this day.

CHAPTER 12

What We Hunted

My father bought me a .410 Stevens shotgun, bolt-action, when I was twelve years old. It was the only gun in the house. It held one shell in the chamber and four in reserve, but we never put more than one in at a time. More than that, and you'd want to shoot up all your shells like a spendthrift. All it ever killed were squirrels and the occasional robin or dove, and it was never fired at a deer, a rabbit, a possum, a coon, or a bobcat. Not that my father and I wouldn't have fired at anything that moved, particularly if it was edible. Though we wanted more protein-bearing wildlife, squirrels and birds were all we ever saw in the logged-out woods in walking distance of where we lived on Farm to Market 1276.

The .410 was technically mine, and it was always referred to as *Gerald's shotgun*, but my father used it much more than I did. I learned soon in the halls of Livingston High School that the gun I owned was not worth mentioning when talk turned to weaponry. You had to have at least a .20 gauge to open your mouth when the topic of firepower was raised, and the preferred piece was an automatic .12 gauge, so powerful it hurt your shoulder each time you set it off.

I remember once standing on a street corner in Livingston and seeing Manson Mathis ride by on his Schwinn bicycle, a bluesteel double-barrel Remington .12 gauge balanced across his basket. I'd never have that firepower, and I knew it. When I fired the .410 I could barely hear it go off, and the pattern of shot it left was random, unchoked, and scattered.

I knew about the sorriness of the .410 pattern because once my father had me lean a piece of discarded plywood up against a tree in the front yard of a recently abandoned farmhouse so he could demonstrate what my shotgun would do. I did that, he wasted a shell in the experiment, and the only interesting thing that happened was that a cat left behind by the departing family chanced to be in the way and was killed by the .410 shot pattern.

"Well, Gerald," my father said, looking down at the cat in its last throes in the high weeds before us, "this piece is not choked down enough to carry much of a kick, but that .410 shell sure took care of this booster." I had to agree, but I knew I couldn't tell my mother about what we'd done, intentional or not. She liked cats.

So we hunted, Big Willie and I did, off and on for the years we lived in the ruined woods near Camp Ruby, but our expeditions were nothing like what I read about later in Hemingway's short stories and Faulkner's mythic accounts of the meaningful slaughter of deer and bear. No level of symbol or patterns of analogy obtained in our excursions into the cut-over pine barrens surrounding us, as we carried the Stevens .410 and four or five shells in support of our mission into the wilderness.

We went out looking to kill squirrels, to skin and gut them, and to take their bodies home for my mother to fry or stew with dumplings. If we didn't see anything worth the expenditure of a shell, we didn't shoot the gun. I remember once spending most of a scalding August day climbing fences, picking our way through briar thickets and yaupon bushes and saplings, studying the tops of loblolly pines for possible movement of any animal, and carrying as ammunition only two shells. That's all we had left in supply, and we returned home with both shells unfired.

Our biggest and best hunt was the one in which we discovered eleven squirrels in one hardwood tree, an oak, standing in the middle of an abandoned house place, far enough away from any other tree that no squirrel might jump for escape from the killing ground. I know there were eleven squirrels at bay that afternoon because my father shot them out of the oak until not a one was left. It took several minutes, but we got every bit of meat out of that tree, my job during the process being to walk around and around the bole to scare the squirrels into revealing themselves to my father and the mighty .410.

I don't remember eating any of those—I didn't like squirrel meat anyway, since it was shot in the woods and I was always so particular about food and everything else, as I was told daily by all around me—but I remember the look on my mother's face that day when we came into the house loaded with the bloody carcasses. Joy. Pleasure. Ease and the certitude of a woman with enough meat to work with to feed the whole family, even if her son would just play with the fried hindquarter on his plate.

So the hunting my father and I did in Polk County was not romantic, not meaningful, not an establishing of bonds between males or between father and son, yet the last time I saw my father alive, some forty years later as he lay blind in the bed of a nursing home in Livingston, his heft and presence eaten away by cancer, unable to speak beyond a whisper, all I could think of to say to him in our last moments ever to be together was thanks for taking me hunting and for reading stories to me when I was young.

I leaned forward, kissed him on the forehead, and told him I loved him, a thing I had not done since childhood. The smell of him I remembered from my youth was not there any longer, he sipped water through a straw rather than drinking from the rim of a glass, and as I left his room, he pulled at a spread to cover his chest because he was cold, blistering summer day though it was. All these signs I recognized to be of weakness and imminent death, and outside in the parking lot of the nursing home I sat beside my sister in the car, crying bitterly aloud at the fact that I had seen my father brought low, as I had always wanted him to be when I lived with him as a child. I finally had what I wanted now, and its taste was not what I expected.

Nancy watched me weep with an expression of deep satisfaction on her face, glad I had been humbled like our dying father, though she didn't speak of the matter and neither did I. Big Willie Duff was gone from my life in fact, though he exists still in dreams that recurrently visit and haunt me. He does not leave me alone. He continues to forgive me, and I have not to this day been able to do the same for him, his blessing and my curse.

When we lived in Nederland in the days before my father had lost his place at the Sun Oil Company, we ate beef and pork roasts, fried chicken on Sundays, pies baked by my mother, ice cream packed by hand (usually a version called tutti frutti, a mixture of nuts and cherries and assorted other sweet bits which I didn't like but ate some of, anyway. It was ice cream, after all). There were also yeast rolls, banana pudding, salads of lettuce and tomatoes and mayonnaise, biscuits with ham and bacon, potato salad, and more of the fare open to purchase by a working man's wages on the Gulf Coast of Texas where all that oil was refined.

When we moved to Polk County after the fall from Eden, we ate fatback, butter beans, pole beans, pinto beans, navy beans, field peas, gravy made from the fried fatback, and any other excess vegetables in season and given to us by truck-farming relatives. You could measure precisely where in the social scale we were by calorie count and fat percentage in the family diet, though such indicators were not much recognized in mid-century. Among her tasks, my mother had that of going from grocery store to grocery store to ask for credit for what could make up the raw materials for what she would be able to put on the table for us. "My husband's temporarily out of work," she would say, "maybe you know him. Willie Duff?"

"Willie. Sure, I thought he had a good job down around Beaumont."

"He did. We're living here now. I just need some flour and sugar and coffee and a few other things. For us and the children."

Humiliation was a constant companion. Once I was sent next door to Aunt Rosalie's house to borrow four slices of light bread to make sandwiches for mine and my sister's school lunch for the next day. My father's sister met me at the door, staring through her glasses at me as though she didn't know who I was.

"Mama told me to ask you if she could borrow some bread to make sandwiches," I said, trying to look Aunt Rosalie in the eyes and not being able to do so for two reasons. The first was that the light was reflected off her lenses in such a way that I couldn't see her eyes, and the second was that I couldn't make myself look steadily at her, my gaze continuing to slide off her face as my head sank lower and lower as she fixed me with her stare.

"Why does Dorothy want to make sandwiches?" she said. "Doesn't she have any cornmeal or flour to make her own bread?"

"For lunch at school," I said. "For me and Nancy to take to school tomorrow."

"Does she think I'm made of bread, Gerald?"

"No, ma'am," I said, looking desperately at the flower pattern in Aunt Rosalie's dress. "She doesn't think that."

"All right," she said. "Come on back here in the kitchen, then. I'll get you some bread, but you got to take the heels from that loaf of Mrs. Baird's bread I got back there. And I want you to remember I gave you this bread for you and Nancy to have sandwiches at school tomorrow. Don't you ever forget it."

I never did. I put Aunt Rosalie in my second novel, in fact, along with her children, and I gave her a featured role, presenting her as a woman convinced she had visitors from outer space and giving her an ongoing case of gastric distress which caused her character to pray aloud to Jesus for some relief from the pressure of indigestion eternally plaguing her.

"Sweet Infant Child of God," her character would beg, "let me belch and get me some solace from the way my food just festers on me. Jesus, hold my hand, let me live, and let me get some of this gas out of me, if it be Thy blessed will."

Work on it, Aunt Rosalie. Cough up that Mrs. Baird's bread, I would think as I scribbled away in Gambier, Ohio, with my Scripto pencil all those years later. *Help her, Sweet Jesus. Here's to you, heel of bread and smear of peanut butter. Do your appointed work.*

Food and its absence and ways to get some of it were with the Willie Duff family day and night in Polk County, Texas, in that time.

CHAPTER 13

Take, Eat, This Is My Body

My first meal in the school cafeteria in Livingston, after we had moved there from the Gulf Coast, introduced me to another truth involving what I ate and how I ate it. I learned something new about the power and significance of food that midday as I stared into my plate among the other low school students of the Livingston Texas Independent School District.

What you ate, I learned that day, was not simply fuel for the functioning of the body and a concurrent response to hunger pangs which came in an orderly pattern easy to anticipate and readily handled. What food meant became immensely more meaningful than it had been in the petro-chemical area of the Texas coast, where everybody's father had a job and everybody's mother had something to throw into a skillet or a pot or an oven each day that rolled.

In Nederland, you ate because you were hungry and food was there to satisfy the need. In deep East Texas amid the pine barrens, people gathered regularly around tables, too, but their manner of address and approach to the plates before them was fraught with meaning. My introduction to that fact took place as I sat in the cafeteria that noon between Joe Baxley and Onita Davis and readied myself to do something about being hungry.

All that was on the plate before me, identical in every way to everyone else's around me, has fled my memory, except for two items, and those two parts of my meal I can still call up at any moment, and will be able to do so on my deathbed. One was a slice of store-bought bread lying by my left hand, and the other was a mound of green English peas, just at room temperature, spooned up and deposited at about two o'clock on the plate.

I immediately lifted the bread to my mouth, took a bite of that, and then added a scoop of the English peas. At that moment, I noticed that none of the third-graders around me had touched the food before them, and I heard our teacher, Mrs. Amerine, say, "Pupils, bow your heads and let us give thanks to God for what He has provided us."

I didn't begin chewing the bread and peas as the teacher's prayer went on, instead letting them lie in my mouth like a stone I had put there by accident, and I stared at the place on the slice of bread where my teeth had removed a portion, leaving an exact replica of my bite mark, the true and inescapable evidence of my transgression. When the prayer was finished, and the rest of the Livingston low school pupils began to tuck in, I chewed the wad of peas and bread already in my mouth, softened and tasteless and hard to swallow as it had become, unblessed and unconsecrated, and not fuel at all but a sign of my shame and ineptitude at eating properly. It went down my gullet like wire.

So that first meal in the public school cafeteria of Livingston, Texas, was my introduction to food as emblem of something larger than itself, symbolic by its presence, or absence, and kind and quality, of a moral dimension to consumption, a commentary on the level of worth and the essential identity of its eater. What I ate and how I ate it, I learned at that moment as I sat, head bowed, the peas and bread liquefying between my unmoving jaws, could and would mark me, set me apart, let the world know my true self, and curse me for the character which my food gave me.

When eating was public, it was an announcement of social placement and access to the funding necessary to support it. What you raised to your mouth spoke volumes, loud and well. People in the Livingston public schools watched you eat, noted the identity of what you put in your mouth, calculated portion size and appearance, and made pronouncement about the proper interpretation of the evidence before them.

"Look what Donald Lowe's eating," I heard Bill Avery say on one of the early days of my time in Polk County, "that's pure dee fatback on his sandwich."

"Naw," John Gardner chimed in with delight, "that's lard smeared on Donald's bread. You can see where his mama's left old burned-up hog hide in it."

The conversation went downhill from there, but it was informative enough to let me know never to bring a lunch to school that wasn't up to Polk County socio-economic standards. Sandwiches had to be on store-bought bread, their contents—if meat—had to be from uniformly sliced prefab chunks, and wrappings had to be waxpaper, not recycled packaging of any sort.

That presented me with problems more than once, resulting chiefly from the habitual shortage of store-bought, pre-sliced Mrs. Baird's or Ideal bread in the Duff household of Camp Ruby. Breadstuff in that place was biscuits on a good day, cornbread at the times necessary to take a step down from wheat flour, and at the bottom of the bread scale was what my mother called fritters.

Fritters now cost top-dollar in many of the restaurants, bistros, and fern bars of American dining establishments, though they aren't called that any more. I've seen the terms *hoe-cake* and *cornbread wrap* and *country flapjacks* applied to these conveyors of cholesterol and fat, but in the Eisenhower years in East Texas, they were simply, flatly and shamefacedly *fritters*. Cornmeal mixed with water and salt, fried in lard on a hot surface, and fated never to rise a quarter of an inch above their original height, given the absence of any leavening.

The taste was minimal, the grease was insistent, and the need to eat them hot was crucial. They filled one function, and that was all they were designed to do. Once delivered, the fritter lay in the belly like a stone.

"More fritters," my sister would lament, interpreting for all of us the pop of the cornmeal patties hitting the frying pan, as though none of us could know what that sound and that smell might mean. We knew it, though, and we knew deeply the truths announced by the breadstuff about to be put before us. The bottom of the food scale had been reached again, and there wasn't anywhere to go in a southerly direction from here except to nothing.

But we ate the fritters, and we drank the water from the well, and when all that was available to take to the cafeteria of the Livingston schools was fritters, we took nothing. To be seen eating such muck as fritters would have been the final and truest branding of just where we ranked in the exquisitely demarcated social strata of Polk County.

My mother knew better than to try to send me off to the halls of learning in East Texas with fritters in my brown paper bag, but once she prepared a biscuit and ham combo for me to have to eat in front of others in my school. Despite my loud protests, she forced me through sheer will to take the offending bag with me to the place in front of our house on Farm to Market Road 1276 where the school bus stopped to pick us up each morning, watching me all the way until I got aboard. As far as she knew, I had the lunch of biscuits and ham safely accompanying me, and I would have it to eat when the lunch hour rolled around. What she couldn't see was my throwing the bag out the window of the school bus when Cary Williams, driver of bus number twelve, left the hard road to go pick up the Hances living a couple of miles off the highway. My proposed lunch hit hard, bounced once, and its motion died in a patch of green.

I could plainly see the bag lying in the rank weeds of the ditch beside the red clay road to the Hance place, but when we returned at the end of the day to let that bunch off, all that was left of the shameful home-cooked biscuits and ham was the bag itself, torn into bits by some hungry animal unbothered by symbolism in the way I had learned to be. Things to me were never simply themselves, objects in the sensible world with no meaning beyond mere existence. No, I had learned through long repetition that things meant and they meant strongly. What they were in themselves was always secondary to what people believed they implied.

Nothing merely lay there, mute and solid. It spoke, it revealed truth, and it betrayed.

At lunch that day, Clarence Whitehead asked me why I didn't go into the cafeteria to eat, and I told him I had forgotten to bring my quarter for the plate lunch sold by the Livingston Independent School District. "They'll let you bring the quarter tomorrow to pay for it," Clarence said, a fact I knew but of no use to me. Clarence was lucky, living right in Livingston and having a part-time job in the newsstand on David Crockett Street, and besides that his mother had regular and continuing employment in the dime store. Easy for *him* to say he'd pay tomorrow when funds became available.

While others ate, I stood outside the cafeteria that day, as I always did when the symbolic and literal meaning of things dictated I do so, listening to Curtis Platt talk about what he'd like to do to Martha Vick. I eagerly agreed with and applauded all Curtis said about his mania, claiming the exact desires he expressed, but knowing my chance of realizing them were as slim as that of being able to buy the plate lunch every day in the Livingston school cafeteria.

"If Martha would let me stick it in her for a dollar, and I had a dollar," Curtis said, "I'd do it and I wouldn't never pull it out, no matter what she said."

"Yeah," I said, "just leave it right there until it thundered."

"Thundered?" Curtis said, a year older than I was and that much further along in understanding need and ways to accommodate it. "What the hell does thunder have to do with pussy?"

"Well, you know," I said, "turtles don't let go until it thunders."

"Crazy asshole," Curtis Platt defined me, and I slunk off to drink out of the water fountain until my belly felt full. But I had not been seen eating biscuits and ham brought from home in a brown paper bag. That set of items had not been allowed to speak, and the nothing that was left and that spoke in itself was an absence I was always ready and able to explain. I could put a twist on that nothing and make it possible to live with, and I cleaved to that tactic like the turtle fearing a fatal clap of thunder. Don't let go, don't let go until something makes you lose that rescuing hold. Make a virtue of nothing and stick to it, no matter what.

CHAPTER 14

Kissing Linda Smith and Loving Jannis Jones

THE FIRST REAL ATTRACTION I FELT TOWARD A PARTICULAR GIRL, APART FROM that session lying on Dolly Roberts's bed as she babysat me at age five when the strange fascination with her legs seized me, was in the fourth grade in Livingston when I came to believe that Linda Lee Smith should be mine. She had long dark hair, ran around the schoolyard in a precise gait, and once let me kiss her on the cheek during a game of tag. I denied that to Mrs. Amerine after one of my classmates had turned informant, knowing what I had done was much too exciting to be permitted by the authorities. I lied so persuasively to my teacher that I almost wept, tears standing in my eyes and my stutter in full gallop.

"You're much too nice a boy to be doing that, Gerald," Mrs. Amerine told me. "That's a nasty thing, and you're much too smart to want to act that way." I assured her I agreed fully with those sentiments, and Linda Lee covered for me, denying anything had happened except that I had caught her in the game and she had become *it*.

I knew that I was not nice, and I was not too smart, and I wanted to be as nasty as the rest of the boys, but I couldn't tell the grown-ups that. I made too many As on my report card to be able to behave like other boys.

So I listened to the nasty jokes from Joe Baxley and Ben Royden at recess, I learned that babies were not delivered by the stork but came from the doctor sticking his thing in women who came to his office for checkups, and I lusted steadily after Linda Lee Smith. All that was in the fourth grade, and by the time I was a fifth grader, I learned that the doctor was off the hook. Instead of the medico, children's parents did that nasty thing which caused babies, Linda Lee Smith was out of my league, and I would never have her as a girlfriend.

I also learned that the Boy Scouts in Troop 53 in Livingston were not dedicated to living by the Scout Law, to learning woodcraft, and how to survive in the wilderness, but were committed instead to jacking off and seeing who could do it the most often and shoot his seed the greatest distance. Rayford was champion of that, blasting his essence all the way across the tent.

The only girl I was ever to come close to in those years was my immediate neighbor, Jannis Jones, lovely in her own right, but convinced that we were simply great pals who played board games together. She saw no difference between her relationship with my sister Nancy and the one with me. It didn't matter to her that I was a boy and she was a girl. Jannis just liked me, and I have never forgiven her for that. At the time, I didn't know what a Platonic relationship was, but I could have defined it in precise and painful detail as I studied each contour of the physical structure that made up Jannis.

Jannis did take off her T-shirt in front of me once when we were hiding together in high weeds during a game of hide-and-seek. She had started to grow nipples which showed through her clothes, and as I knelt in the blast of summer heat beside her, I knew she wanted me to look at her breasts and see what she had been up to lately. Gutless, I couldn't force myself to look away from the cluster of weed stems immediately before me, and I lost the chance. In a minute or so, Jannis put her shirt back on, we rejoined the others, and after that time I never played much with her again. In high school, she ended up going steady with John, son of the local physician, a Livingston Lions football player, and a person so self-possessed he would tear pieces of paper off his in-class compositions and stuff them in his mouth, chewing away steadily in complete composure as he delivered his oral reports. They married eventually, had children, divorced, and having learned to hate each other, refused ever to attend reunions of the class of 1957 at the same time.

CHAPTER 15

Leaving for Marshall Hall

In the summer of 1954 at age fifteen, I got on a Trailways bus at the station in Livingston, headed for Washington, DC, and accompanied by a brown tin suitcase containing all my clothes and a set of sheets. My mother's brother, Uncle Roderick Irwin, aka Hooky, had the food concessions at Marshall Hall Amusement Park on the Potomac, south of DC and just across from Mount Vernon, George's home. Uncle Roderick subsidized my bus ticket and twenty dollars for food money, and all he wanted in return was for me to work seven days a week from nine AM until eleven PM in the Round Stand selling hot dogs, sodas, and ice cream cones to the patrons who rode the excursion boat, the *Mount Vernon*, down the river from DC to Marshall Hall, and to the locals from Southern Maryland.

Workers in the park did get Monday nights off. We slept in the mansion built by John Marshall in 1690, we ate free in the restaurant specially prepared meals for workers, and I was paid twenty-five dollars a week. My uncle kept the bulk of my salary for me, and issued me a check at the end of the summer when I would take another bus back to Texas. I jumped at the chance to be there, and I worked in the Round Stand for four summers.

What was not to like? Except for my uncle, the worst boss I was ever to have in my entire life, the ninety-two hour workweek, the many thousands of hot dogs and ice cream cones cooked and dipped and sold by me, and the tourists from DC who professed not to understand my accent. But it beat spending my teenage summers in East Texas, eating fritters and crowder peas, and it got me away from my Duff kin.

At Marshall Hall, there was plenty to eat, supplemented by the hot dogs and ice cream I stole (all workers were supposed to pay for all we ate and none did, justifying our theft by the way Hooky Irwin raged at us, called us names, sneaked around to catch us not standing even when there were not any customers to serve, never spoke a word to any employee except to criticize, and paid us twenty-seven cents an hour). There was a room of my own to sleep in, there were new and strange people to meet, and in particular there was my cousin Addison.

Addison was four years older than I was. He had just graduated from a military high school in South Carolina called Carlisle Academy, and he owned a brand new car from England called a Hillman Minx. Addison would be going to college in the fall, he had a steady girlfriend named Jeanie back in South Carolina (he didn't let that stop him from dating other ones in Maryland, though), and he treated me as though he liked me. He introduced me to a new world.

Getting to Marshall Hall from Polk County, Texas, required a two-day bus ride, with rest stops and bus changes and ticket reissues (the clerk in Livingston had no idea how to navigate me across eight states cleanly), and the trip provided me with all the material I needed for getting the American Indian protagonist of my first novel, Sam Houston Leaping Deer, from Texas to Illinois twenty years later.

My uncle had told me in his letter of instruction for the trip to Marshall Hall to get a taxi when I arrived in Washington, tell the driver I wanted to go to the Wilson Lines Dock at the Seventh Street Wharves, and tell the people there to let me ride the excursion boat, the *Mount Vernon*, down the Potomac to Marshall Hall. I memorized those instructions, said them to myself over and over, and on my deathbed, if someone asks me to repeat them, I will be able to respond correctly, no matter how befogged I may be by drugs and the impending end of my consciousness of self and this world. I was determined in May of 1954 not to get lost and to get to where I was supposed to arrive.

On my way, I had an encounter and witnessed an episode in the bus station in Jackson, Mississippi, that captured a side of human behavior I would use in that first novel *Indian Giver*. It began in the Trailways men's room, one larger and more magnificent than any I had seen before.

"Damn it," a man at the urinal next to mine said. "I hate this waiting worse than anything." No one else relieving themselves responded to the remark, keeping their heads down, so I thought I should probably answer, say something in acknowledgment. After all, the man was dressed in a dark suit, white shirt, wearing a tie, and I was raised to be polite. His shoes were worn, though, and he needed a haircut, a wad of well-oiled locks hanging a little long over his collar.

"I know what you mean," I said. "Waiting for a bus sure is boring."

"I ain't waiting for a goddamned bus," the man said bitterly. "I'm talking about waiting for pussy."

I zipped up and left the fancy men's room in a hurry, and I began watching the man in the dark suit closely after he came out and took a seat in one of the rows for waiting. I noticed he had a deformed right hand, only one or two fingerlike appendages evident, and for some reason that took on great significance for me. I had seen several men and at least one woman with missing fingers in East Texas already, of course. That was logging country, and losing fingers and other parts of the body was a hazard the people I lived among suffered from. It was not unusual not to be all there.

The shortage the Jackson, Mississippi, man waiting for pussy suffered was different, though. It spoke to me of a deeper gap in his makeup, something missing from birth, something a person needed to possess to be able to function properly around other people. I watched him carefully, noted his rundown shoes, his ragged haircut, the paleness of his face, his wearing of a tie out of keeping with every other male in the building—save for the ticket clerks, bus drivers, and black porters pushing carts loaded with suitcases and bundles and boxes wrapped in brown paper, all sporting some kind of tie as part of the uniform.

I noted that he kept turning to look up into a balcony area above the main waiting room, where a door was marked Ladies and several sofa-like chairs were located for ladies to use. One of them held a woman, who may have been wearing a small hat, though my memory is not clear on that possibility, but she was well-dressed. She had on a flowered dress, high-heeled shoes, costume jewelry of some sort, and she was looking at a magazine. Now and then, though, I noticed her looking down from her seat in the balcony for ladies toward the man craning his neck to peer up at her. She looked away whenever she saw him looking at her, and she was only pretending to read her magazine, I was convinced. She was not smiling, but the man with the deformed hand lifted one side of his mouth each time their eyes met.

He was not really smiling to be friendly, I judged, but in the way you might move your lips when you were sitting down at a table set for dinner. The woman in the flowered dress was the pussy for which the man in the dark suit waited.

When the announcement came to board our bus, the woman gathered her belongings; she must have had a purse and a bag, but all I remember was the magazine she rolled up, and came down the stairs from the ladies balcony. The man missing part of his hand stood up and moved to the foot of the stairs and said something to the woman as she passed, shrinking against the handrail as she went by.

As people began to board the bus, I followed immediately behind the man in the dark suit and ruined shoes, who had let another person step in between him and the woman on whom he waited. When she reached the bus driver standing by the door checking ticket stubs, the woman leaned close to him and said something, words which it took her longer to say than it would have if they had been a question about the bus schedule. The driver looked up at the man behind her, a man in khaki pants, a short-sleeved shirt, and a straw hat, and I heard the woman speak.

"Not him," she said, nodding toward the man behind, the one before me, the man missing part of himself.

The woman went up the steps of the bus, the man in khaki following, and the bus driver motioned to the man in front of me, the man waiting on pussy, to step aside to listen. "This lady tells me you've been bothering her," the bus driver said.

"Who, me?" the man answered, and what most surprised me was not his lying, but the whine in his voice. It spoke to me of weakness, fear, and a refusal to back up an assertion he had strongly proclaimed. "I don't know what she's talking about. I don't even know that lady."

"Listen, you son of a bitch," the driver said in a low voice, "I'm going to let you get on the bus, but you're going to sit in the back. And if you say a word to her, I'll put you off wherever we happen to be at the time, I don't give a damn where."

That's all I remember. I'm sure I noted where the woman sat on the bus, which seat the man missing part of himself was relegated to, and where I sat in relation to the two of them, but the final part of the episode which lasts in my memory was a great sense of relief at the bus driver's exercise of authority in face of the man's declared intention toward the woman, mixed with my sense that at least a postponement of the darkness associated with a ruined man's enslavement to what he called pussy had been granted me.

The man with the missing part was not a revelation to me of what might await me when I ventured away from the familiar and went into the darkness alone. At that point, I had never heard or read the word *epiphany*, but later on when I learned its definition I realized that back in 1954 in Jackson, Mississippi, I had glimpsed the possibility of experiencing a revelation that I did not want. I had not endured an epiphany but an absence of one. Maybe that was an epiphany in itself.

In Washington, the man at the desk in the office of the Wilson Lines at the Seventh Street Wharves could not comprehend at first what I wanted when I asked for passage to Marshall Hall for me and my brown tin suitcase.

"You're not trying to buy a ticket?" he asked. "You don't want to go to Marshall Hall on the boat and come back tonight?"

"No sir," I said. "My uncle Roderick Irwin didn't say anything about buying a ticket. He just said I should take the boat down the river and get off at Marshall Hall."

"You're not on a senior trip to DC? Why are you carrying that suitcase?"

"It's got my clothes in it," I said, leaving out the fact that it also contained two sheets. "I'm going to work there."

He was reluctant, but he spoke to somebody else who told me where to go, and after a while I found myself walking up the gangplank in the midst of a group of boys and girls older than I was, and much unlike me in dress, appearance, and mood. They were laughing, poking at each other, speaking in strange tones and accents, threatening good-naturedly to throw various ones of them in the water, and now and then giving me and my suitcase puzzled and sardonic looks.

Darkness came soon after the *Mt. Vernon* left the dock. A band on the boat played music while several people sang into microphones, people danced in various kinds of patterns and steps, and I bought myself a Coke and watched, my suitcase always close enough for me to keep an eye on it. The one song they played impressive enough for me to remember was "Standing on the Corner, Watching All the Girls Go By," and as I sipped at my Coke and watched the young people from Washington, DC, glide about the dance floor of the excursion boat in their colorful clothes to that tune, I considered that I had arrived at the big time. I was being granted a glimpse at civilization.

When we arrived over an hour later, the trip up the dock at Marshall Hall itself was filled with bright lights, the sounds of amusement park rides revving their engines, the shrieks of their riders, the clicking of wheels of fortune in the betting stands, the smells of popcorn and burnt sugar. I carried my brown tin suitcase up to a gaudy ticket stand and asked where I should go to find my uncle, aunt, and cousin.

Later I was told by one of the workers in the Round Stand where I was to spend my days for the next four summers that they had all immediately spotted me coming up the cement walk from where the *Mt. Vernon* was docked.

"We knew it was you," Pee Wee LeBlanc said, "just as soon as we saw you. You know how?"

"No. How?"

"It wasn't just that old suitcase," Pee Wee said. "I seen people carrying funnier looking things than that before lots of times. Naw, it was the way you was looking out of your eyes. The way you was jerking your head around. You looked scared to death, yeah."

I wasn't scared, I assured Pee Wee LeBlanc and Boose Fontenot and the other two Cajuns listening. I wasn't scared at all. I just hadn't slept much on the bus, that was what explained it.

But that first night, after they had shown me to my room on the second floor of the Marshall Hall mansion, right next to the one in which three of the Cajun workers stayed, I made sure to lock my door, a thing I had never had occasion to do before in my first fifteen years in Texas. I went to sleep on my new sheets listening to the three occupants in the other room speaking in French, singing snatches of Cajun songs, and from what I could tell, laughing like hyenas in French as well.

CHAPTER 16

Who Is a Cajun and Who Is a Negro?

My uncle and his wife Augustina (Teeny for short) lived in Rayne, Louisiana, her home during the seven months of the year they weren't at Marshall Hall, and Hooky Irwin figured out early on that the way to pay low wages and avoid union problems in Maryland was to hire Cajuns from Southwest Louisiana to work in the restaurant, the bar, and the Round Stand. Plenty of young Cajun men were ready to travel to Maryland for work during that time, at least for a summer or two, and the majority of my uncle's employees were drawn from that group.

It made for an interesting mix, certainly not one I was used to. No one was as young as I was, except for the black kids from Southern Maryland who were hired to roam through the park pushing a cart and picking up soda bottles for return in that pre-plastic product-discard era. A few of the Cajun imports were close to my age—Pee Wee LeBlanc and Charles Boudreau—but most were grown men, unmarried and unskilled and ambitionless in a conventional sense. Others were older men, divorced and used-up and, though I didn't realize it at the time, on the edge of what's now called homelessness.

Everyone was jolly, everyone sang songs in Cajun French, everyone knew how to talk to women, and all took a good-natured interest in me. I was the boss's nephew, after all, though that didn't provide me any special treatment. I was younger than the rest of them, I was utterly ignorant of the world they knew, and most important, I would listen to and believe anything they told me.

All of them worked hard, and most took pride in what they did, pointing out to me how to do a job properly and never to quit until it was finished. When the official from the Maryland State Department of Food Handling, or whatever that agency was called, came unannounced to inspect the facilities for cleanliness and adherence to regulations, Pee Wee and Eldridge and Boose were elated when the inspector pronounced the floors "very nice" and the kitchen conditions in the restaurant "well above average."

Pee Wee LeBlanc walked around for several hours in the Round Stand with a distant look and relaxed smile on his face, repeating aloud three or four times the two magic phrases. "Floors is very nice," he would say. "Kitchen conditions well above average." Then he would punch me on the shoulder and ask, "How you like that, Gerard Petah?"

I asked Pee Wee how to spell the name he called me and what it meant, but he said, "French can't be wrote down, no. English you can write, if you learn it in school, but French you can just talk, not write."

"Yeah, but what does the name mean?" I asked him, knowing full well he was wrong about the writeability of French but careful not to disagree and possibly hurt Pee Wee's feelings. Besides that, I knew he did not easily countenance opposition to a statement he had made.

"It just means your name in French," he said. "It sounds better than in English, yeah. Petah, it means firecracker."

"You think I'm like a firecracker?" I said, taken with the notion.

"No," Pee Wee said, "That's why I call you that."

Every morning, all of us living upstairs in Marshall Hall would get up and go down to the rear of the restaurant, where an industrial sized sink was available to us. We used it for washing up in the morning and for washing our clothes and our work aprons by hand in the course of the day. It was also one of the main places where the Cajuns talked to each other and to me and Richard, one of the black pickers-up of bottles.

Richard was the first black person I ever met and talked to without some other person of my own race present. My father had introduced me to several black men over the years, during his dealings with loggers in particular, so I had heard conversations between whites and blacks that took place, for the most part, on the front porches of houses in the "quarter," as the area was called in Livingston where blacks lived. My father was at ease with black people, as he was with anybody who would listen to him talk, and he worked alongside blacks in the logging woods, partnering with one man in particular as a two-man crosscut saw team.

I would accompany Big Willie Duff when he went to the quarter to let his partner know a job was available, and we would stand around in the yard of the shotgun house where the partner lived, my father and the black sawyer talking and drinking coffee fetched from the house by a woman, his wife I supposed. Once she even brought me a Coke, a treat not readily available for blacks or working class whites either in that place and time.

My only encounter alone with a black person before I knew Richard and

Clarence and Racehorse in Maryland had occurred when, as a five-year-old, I was trying to climb a stile over a fence marking the division of my aunt's property from what everybody called the "nigger quarter." A black woman, known as Old Bertha by the white folks in the area, saw the trouble I was having with the steep stile over the fence, and had the temerity to offer me some help. I ran shrieking for my aunt's house, convinced by what I had absorbed through cultural osmosis that Old Bertha was out to get me.

She ran behind me, trying to calm me down, and—as I realized years later—doing her best to get her story to the white folks at the house before I got my version of events registered. Her trotting along behind me, dressed as she was in many layers of different-colored clothes in the winter weather, and jabbering words at me I couldn't understand, scared me even more, and I was a babbling idiot by the time I got to the steps to Aunt Rosalie's porch. To get me back to some semblance of sanity, it took a lot of soothing by my mother and assurances that Old Bertha was only trying to help me climb the stile.

That was long ago by the time I had my conversations with Richard at the washing-up sink behind the restaurant at Marshall Hall, however, and he and I at about the same age had a lot to say to each other. One morning in particular stood out.

I was looking into the mirror stuck up above the sink, fixing my hair I had wet down for combing, as Richard stood off to the side watching me work to arrange my part and get the stragglers positioned behind my ears.

"Gerald," Richard said, "Let me ask you something. Tell me the truth now."

"What?" I said, not taking my eyes away from what I was doing.

"How come is it that white people got such pretty hair, and colored people ain't?"

"I don't know," I said. "What you mean by 'pretty'?"

"The way your hair is straight, and lays down when you comb it. The way that lets you fix it up pretty with the comb. I can't do that with my hair. It's too kinky. It won't comb."

"I don't know," I said again, acknowledging that Richard was right in his judgment of the comparative beauty of my hair as separate from his. "It just is, I guess."

"The thing is," Richard said, "our blood is just alike. If I cut my finger and you cut your finger, what comes out is red blood, the same from both of us. Ain't that right?"

"Well, I guess so," I admitted, "but blood is blood, and hair is hair. There can't be any difference in blood like it is with hair. Hair can't run, like blood can. Blood is like water."

"It still don't make sense to me," Richard said. "It don't seem like it's fair."

"That's the difference between colored people and white, I suppose," I said to Richard, getting uneasy at the questions he was raising, but knowing that he was right. My hair was prettier and easier to work with than his was. What I didn't like about what Richard was saying was not the truth he had spoken, but the fact that he seemed to resent the hair advantage I had as a white. Why couldn't he just accept that I had a better deal than he did and just go on with his life without complaining about it?

At that time in Southern Maryland, Richard could walk all over the amusement park pushing his cart and picking up bottles to put in it, he could eat with the rest of us in the restaurant at the workers' table, he could and did spend time talking with us and joking around, and he could be seen anywhere on the grounds the rest of us workers might be found. One thing he and his kind could not do, though, was enter Marshall Hall Amusement Park as a patron, ride the rides, buy a hot dog or a Coke, drink out of the water fountains, or spend a cent of American money on the premises.

All of us working the counters, bars, and entrances to the pleasures of Marshall Hall were instructed our first day on the job that we couldn't serve colored people. What was meant by "colored" was clear enough all right. That designation didn't include dark skins from places like India and East Asia or South America and Mexico. It was aimed straight at those with African blood.

All of us accepted that, were comfortable with it, and had no qualms about saying to anyone who looked the part that we didn't serve "Negroes" at Marshall Hall. It so happened that I never had to say that to a real "Negro," though, since all the local blacks in the area had never been in the park as patrons and never expected to be there in that role. They knew their place. That I assumed, anyway.

Only once did I have to challenge the right of a person to buy a hot dog and grape soda from me on the basis of his skin color, and when that occurred I learned immediately I had made a mistake.

The person who asked me for service had come down the Potomac on a night cruise on the *Mt. Vernon*, and he was therefore not local and was much more likely to make the mistake of assuming he could make a purchase at the Round Stand, even though standing there announcing his origins by his color. When the man asked for whatever it was he wanted, I waited patiently until he finished and leaned forward to speak softly so as not to embarrass him by what I had to say. He was well dressed, wearing a light-colored hat and a summer suit, and he had fingernails that glowed in the artificial light of the Round Stand. They were polished. His skin was much darker than Richard's, though, and I could tell he was not eligible for service according to the regulations of Marshall Hall.

"I'm sorry," I said to him after he had given me his order. "We don't serve Negroes."

"Negroes!" he said in a burning tone. "I am not a Negro. I am a member of the Burmese legation to the United States of America, and I demand an apology."

Helpless, I turned to my cousin Addison who happened to be serving someone next to me, and asked what I should do. "He says he's not a Negro."

"Serve him," Addison said, "and tell him you're sorry you made a mistake."

Later, the man served and the transaction completed, I asked Addison what I should do if it happened that someone who truly was a Negro insisted he wasn't when my best judgment told me he was.

"Anybody that says he's not one, you serve him," Addison said. "It's not your job to make somebody admit he's colored. If he doesn't tell the truth, that's his problem to live with, not yours."

"Do many of them claim they're not colored when they really are?" I asked.

"Naw," Pee Wee LeBlanc said, listening in on the conversation and trying to be helpful. "Most niggers will say they're niggers. If a real one won't say he is, it's something wrong with his head."

"Crazy?" I said.

"Crazy," Pee Wee said. "It's no telling what he might do. Stay clear of that fool."

Say what you would about Richard, I realized, he knew what he was and admitted it. What he didn't admit was that he was at ease about what his being colored meant in affecting the things he could and couldn't do. He couldn't go to movie theatres in Maryland, I learned to my amazement.

"Colored folks in Texas can't go to the picture show downstairs where the white people sit," I told Richard. "But they can go in the side door and climb the stairs and sit in the colored balcony."

"And see the same picture shows?" Richard said. "At the same time as the white people watches them?"

"Sure, they just can't come downstairs and sit in the white seats."

"I wish it was that way here. I wouldn't mind sitting upstairs. I'd like it."

"So you never see picture shows then?" I asked, and Richard explained about the colored man in Bryan's Road. "He shows colored picture shows in his house, movies with colored actors playing all the parts, and he charges people money to get in."

"In his house? And the shows have all colored people in them?"

"Sure," Richard said. "They do all the parts, and Mr. Carver, he has a movie projector to show the pictures and play the sound of them talking."

"Not cowboy pictures, though."

"Every kind. Cowboy, war, gangsters, all of it. Colored people do everything white people do, just not so nice."

So Richard let me know about what a black person my age in Maryland might experience in day-to-day life, but Racehorse LeBlanc, who shared a last name with one of the white Cajun workers, a fact which was never remarked upon, was a grown man from Louisiana, though he picked up bottles like Richard, along with doing some heavier lifting. Racehorse interested me most because he supplied stories about his encounters with women to me and Joe

Iserman, a white local boy my age who worked in the Round Stand. My cousin Addison listened to the stories Racehorse told as well, but his sardonic attitude implied that he was an older man of the world himself with no real need to hear what a black man from Louisiana had to say about sex.

Racehorse came up to the Round Stand one day in midweek with only a few customers in the park, bought a Coke from me, and asked me a favor. "Gerald," he said, "I expect you know how to read what people write down by hand, don't you? Because some of it I can't. What's on the newspaper, the way it is there, I can read most all of them words."

I assured Racehorse LeBlanc I could read handwriting as well as printing, and he pulled an envelope out of his pants pocket and handed it to me. "See can you tell me what this here says."

"Who's it from?" I said, reading the name *Polly Deloache* off the return address. "Is this your sister or somebody writing to you?"

"Naw," Racehorse said, taking a sip from his Coke. "I ain't got no sister to write to me. Polly is a girlfriend of mine from Breaux Bridge. I can read that big *P* up there at the front of the name. That's who it is. That's the way she make her name look when she writes it down."

"Dear Lawrence," I began reading aloud, and at that Joe Iserman walked over to listen in. Later he would buy a soda and a hot dog for Racehorse in exchange for being allowed to copy the letter onto another sheet of paper that he could keep. "Lawrence," I said, "Is that your real name?"

"That's the name I give her," Racehorse said. "That's what Polly knows me by."

"I miss you, baby," I read aloud. "Since you been gone, all I know to think about is your sweet loving dick." The letter went on from there, and by the time I had finished reading the entire epistle, Joe and Addison and Bud Pickle, operator of the Rideo located next to the Round Stand, were all standing in close hearing range.

"Read that part again," Bud Pickle said, "where it says about the woman coming all over you."

"How do you make a woman that crazy about you when you doing that to her?" Joe Iserman asked Racehorse. "What makes her want it so bad?"

"Gentlemen," Racehorse announced, "it ain't the meat, it's the motion."

Later that summer, Racehorse Leblanc would go to my uncle, complaining about a physical discomfort which led Hooky Irwin to take his employee to visit a doctor in Bryan's Road, Maryland. The physician diagnosed the ailment as what is today called an STD, but in 1954 had a simpler name, one my cousin Addison would use in a little jingle he sang each time Racehorse would push his bottle cart past the Round Stand.

"I'd rather have the measles than the..." Addison would say and then applaud three times. Racehorse would laugh uproariously each time Addison delivered his chant, and then swear to the efficacy of modern medicine. "They got pills and shots now will cure any ailment," Racehorse would claim. "That make it open season on the wooly booger all the time."

The other black man I got to know at Marshall Hall was Clarence, the head cook at the park restaurant, and he was a settled married man whose wife and child lived with him in a small apartment on the grounds. He had been in the army in Korea, and he still wore his uniform jacket on cool nights when he came down from the restaurant to cook hot dogs on the grill in the Round Stand during the hour-long rush of customers off the boat after the *Mt. Vernon* docked at night at Marshall Hall. Sometimes there were so many customers screaming for hot dogs, soft drinks, and ice cream cones that none of us servers had time to look up from our transactions at the counter, much less tend to the hot dog grill.

Clarence was a man of great dignity who never became flustered during a rush, either in the restaurant kitchen or at the hot dog grill, not even when people were leaning into the Round Stand baying for bread, grease, and sugar, slapping their money on the counter, and demanding something besides the sole condiment we offered for their weenies, mustard cut with white vinegar. The easier the thinned-out mustard poured out of the bottles, the less of the more expensive ingredient customers used, my uncle reasoned, and the fewer choices they had the faster they ordered, laid their money down, and got out of the way for our next victim.

Clarence handled his grilling duties with aplomb, refusing to answer customers' requests or complaints by simply jerking his head in the direction of one of the servers running around the cement floor of the Round Stand, and piling up the grilled hot dogs in neat stacks for us to trade for that money from Washington, DC.

I saw Clarence upset and emotional only once, and I was the cause of the blowup. That occurred one night before the excursion boat had even arrived at the Marshall Hall dock, and none of the Round Stand crew was even working hard yet. I was outside wandering around the park with Joe Iserman. Clarence had stopped for a smoke before going into the building to begin getting the grill fired up and loaded for the rush of customers to come off the boat. He was standing behind the structure in the shadows, out of the lights of the Rideo next to the Round Stand, and Joe Iserman and I could see the glow of his cigarette as Clarence puffed away and then its dimming as he waited before taking another hit of smoke.

"Clarence doesn't see us," Joe whispered as we walked toward the Round Stand. "See how he's got his back turned? Let's see if we can scare him."

I was game for that, and we came up behind the head cook of the restaurant at Marshall Hall on tiptoe and then yelled together at him. What we said I don't remember, and it may have been something as innocuous as "Boo," or a wordless yell. I'll never forget Clarence's response, though. He jumped, spun around in a crouch to his left, and jammed his hand into his pants pocket.

When he saw who we were, he spit his cigarette out and I watched the trail of sparks it made as it fell to the ground behind the Round Stand. He cursed us as little dumb-assed white bastards, and his voice was low, venomous, and grating in a tone I had never heard a grown man use to me before.

"Don't you never come up behind a nigger again like that and try to scare him," Clarence said. "He'll cut your gizzard out and feed it to you."

What shocked me most was not the threat of the violence I might be rewarded with for such a stupid act, but the fact that Clarence had called himself a nigger. Joe and I were not thinking of him as that, and in fact had long ceased to regard Clarence as anything but the head cook at the restaurant who helped us out with the hot dog rush on weekends when the boat from Washington was full of customers.

If someone had asked me if Clarence was what he called himself, I would have readily admitted the accuracy of that classification, but that label for him and for Richard and Racehorse had ceased to have any relevance for me during the time I had come to know them.

Clarence thought of himself as that name at any time he thought he was being treated like that, I realized, and that knowledge was deeply frightening to me. I wanted to say to him that I hadn't tried to scare him because I considered him to be that terrible name, but because I was stupid and I liked him and you played tricks on people you liked. But all I could do, I knew somehow, was not to touch that notion, but to say I was sorry and hadn't meant to disturb him.

The relationship of Clarence to me and Joe Iserman was different from that time forward. We still worked together on good terms, Clarence still helped us out during the night rush in the Round Stand at Marshall Hall, we still talked about any topic that was raised by any of the workers in the hot dog business, but I never again was at ease with Clarence. The fault was not his, I knew. It was not mine by intention, but somehow I had to be careful in a way I had never been before. Immediacy and spontaneity had been killed stone-dead, and I knew that, and I was sorry for the death.

CHAPTER 17

Wanting Some Tongue, Too

BEING AT MARSHALL HALL THE SUMMERS OF 1954 TO 1957 ALLOWED ME TO DO what I couldn't do back home in Texas: go out with girls. At home I had no access to a car—except if I rode along with friends who did. Invitations for that seldom came. I always did all my homework and made As in all my courses, teachers liked me, and I was not able to play any sport well enough to make any team. In Texas, I led a life that doomed me to sexual solitude.

Until the fifth grade, I thought highly of myself. In the fourth grade, I had been the leader of a bunch who called themselves Gerald's gang, and I had kissed Linda Lee Smith during recess and was acknowledged by my classmates to be romantically linked to her.

Then something happened in the summer between the fourth and fifth grades. A gap opened up in the way I thought about myself and the way I fit in with other people. I know precisely when I realized that a hole in my life existed and that it meant I didn't know how to act anymore. The revelation was sudden, it was hard, and it lasted.

It was a blustery day in Livingston, Texas, sometime late in the year right before Christmas. A norther had blown down from the plains and swept into East Texas, and it was cold enough that a bunch of us had gathered in the vestibule of the school building at recess to get in out of the blast.

Several boys and two or three girls were huddled together, not allowed to go back in the building until the bell rang, and I was one of these, standing near Linda Lee Smith but not right by her. Attempting to remedy that, since I considered myself her boyfriend, I moved toward her and was cut off by some other boy. He deliberately moved between the two of us and stared me straight in the eye with a look of challenge. I felt drained of will, my ears rang, and I failed the test, dropping my gaze and allowing him to move up to stand by Linda. Deep in my belly something began to coil and twist into a knot. It hardened and settled and stayed. And I knew I had better get used to it, since it had found its fit home for good.

I did not deserve to stand close to Linda Lee Smith, I came to know in that brick vestibule leading from the Livingston Elementary School building with the cold wind from up north whipping around me. The ground I had once had for asserting myself had somehow crumbled away, and I had not noticed that loss, but now that I did it was real and true and all I could think about.

And thinking too much about what bothered or scared me had always been my downfall, and I knew the more I did not want to think about a thing the more that I would. I could not act. I could not exist without a consciousness of how the world would judge my action. I would know too much, and I would feel the knowledge too sharply. Not the event itself, which could not last in time, but the knowledge of how it could be interpreted, which would last forever, was what tortured me.

So leaving Texas where all those around had me classified, placed, and dismissed offered me the chance to be new in a different place. People there might not care to know me or be around me or acknowledge me, but crucial for me was the fact that no one in Maryland in those four summers would have already figured me out and put me in that place in that deadening system where I truly belonged. In Maryland, I could lie boldly and at will about who I was and wasn't, and there was a possibility that somebody might be fooled into believing me. Denying the truth might save me after all.

In my favor was the fact that the girls who worked in the park or had connections there didn't know me. I wasn't enrolled in school and didn't have to make As in all my classes and bear the isolation that might bring, and I wasn't expected to have access to a car since I was from out of state and working in the Round Stand only for the season. I could approach girls with dating as my intent, and no one would note my inappropriateness for such socio-sexual activity. I wouldn't be immediately and automatically disqualified by my known identity. Maybe I could cut one or two of the weak ones out of the herd.

Things did move in slow stages, though, and I didn't just suddenly find myself endowed with full-blown charm and confidence. I wouldn't be able to simply walk up to an age-appropriate female, and say *hey, baby, let's pair off*. There was a period of study and meditation for me to get through, mainly involving watching my older cousin Addison operate around females and listening to what he told me about them in the same manner an untried fighter pilot would soak up all he could from a veteran of many dogfights hidden in the perilous clouds.

"A girl will like for you to make her laugh," he said. "You have to be bold. Never ask if you can do something. Just go ahead and try, and she'll let you know how far you can take it. Don't worry about that."

"Won't she get mad if you try to kiss her or grab her and she doesn't want to?" I said.

"No," Addison would say, puffing away thoughtfully at his cigarette as we leaned up against the Round Stand counter, watching patrons of Marshall Hall wandering by and hoping to spot a good-looking one in the mix. "She'll expect that, and it won't bother her. What will bother her is if you just sit there like a bump not doing anything. All of them, Gerald, no matter how pretty or ugly or skinny or fat know what you're after, and if you show them you know they know what you want and you're coming after it, they'll know just how to act. You don't want to do anything to puzzle them."

"Puzzle them?"

"Yeah, puzzle them. Act like you don't know what's going on. They hate that shit."

I didn't write any of Addison's admonitions and tips down for later study, since I instantaneously engraved somewhere in my prefrontal lobe all he uttered at the moment he said it. But I bided my time and waited until a moment of ripeness would arrive. The first of these involved a girl, in my mind a full-grown woman, of seventeen or eighteen who sold ride tickets from a booth not far from the Round Stand.

She worked alone in the booth and was forbidden to leave her post until her replacement arrived to give her a break or to take over the booth at the end of her shift. When she would lean back in the booth, I could see her outline from her waist up, and I had been much taken for days with her profile, particularly her lower lip which protruded much more than that of an ordinary woman. She was out of my league in many ways, age difference aside. Grown men in the park hung around her booth so much so that the park manager had put word out that she was not to be bothered while she worked. I had seen her on breaks walking with an assortment of men, and I suspected in my heart of hearts that she was a woman who had done it, was doing it on a regular basis, and liked doing it.

Watching her during a slack period of hot dog and soda-selling one day, I was surprised to see her waving at me, not only waving but gesturing with one hand for me to come to her booth. I pointed at my chest and put on an expression of what I intended to be cool inquisitiveness, to which she nodded her head and gestured once more.

By the time I'd left the Round Stand for her booth, I had decided that here was my chance to make some kind of advance to the woman, what I didn't know, but I could tell she was going to ask me for something. A transaction was about to take place, and I had to get fair return for giving her whatever she wanted.

"No," she said as I put my face up to the ticket slot. "Come around to the side door. I'll open it. I can't leave for another hour, and I'm dying for an orange drink. Will you bring me one if I give you the money right now?"

"Sure," I said, wondering what I was going to ask in return and then hearing myself go on to say, "if you'll give me a kiss."

She drew back a bit, and then seemed to relax. "OK," she said. "But only when you get back here with the orange soda."

I was back in less than a minute, carrying an orange drink which I had dug out from the box deep under the ice. It was frigid, and since we didn't sell many orange or grape drinks, it had been iced down long enough that deposits of frost were sticking to the bottle all the way up.

"All right," she said, taking the bottle, "you're Gerald, right?"

"Yeah," I said, leaning into the booth through the side door.

"I guess you're going to want some tongue, too, aren't you?" she said in a resigned tone, and though not ever having that in my mind, I stuttered out agreement.

The kiss lasted only a second or two, but she did lean forward, turned her head to meet my lips and touched just the tip of her tongue to mine.

"Anytime you want some more orange drinks, just let me know."

"I probably won't need to ask you again," she said. "Today there ain't no other ticket girls around."

I left to go back to the Round Stand, every receptor in my head buzzing, telling myself that Addison was right. Girls didn't mind if you let them know what you wanted. They might not let you have it, but they didn't get mad at you for asking. I knew I'd never forget the way that full lower lip felt right before the tongue did its part. To this day I have not.

If the ticket booth tongue woman was the appetizer, Jeanie B became my first main course. Not that I ever considered being able to enjoy the full entrée, but I devoted myself to nibbling around the edges.

Jeanie B was the niece of the park policeman. She frequently came down from Havre de Grace to visit Officer Jim and his wife, and she was beautiful. At least four-fifths of her was. The parts that were beautiful were her face, her hair, her abundant breasts, and her eagerness to be around males. What was problematic was the fact that Jeanie B had suffered from an attack of polio as a child that left her with one leg substantially smaller than the other and a pronounced limp. When she walked, she listed badly to one side at each step, clumping along on a built-up shoe.

In my mind, that made her the weak one of the herd that I should be able to cut out for approach. The time was the 1950s. I was a teenager with hormones raging through my system, and I didn't feel guilty about attempting to take advantage of her situation until many years later in the coolly contemplative days of adulthood shaped by my days in college and graduate school and teaching in universities. It was easy at that later time to realize what an oafish and unfeeling creature I had been in those Marshall Hall days, but being around Jeanie B in my callow youth blinded me to such considerations.

She was beautiful, she told me she loved me, and she let me kiss her in the backseat of Addison's Hillman Minx until my lips went numb and I suffered my first case of blue balls, a frequent malady claimed at the time and one I was elated to be able to experience, too. Addison in the front seat of the parked Hillman was getting down to much more serious business with his date, I knew, but I was satisfied to make out with Jeanie B, wallow around on her large endowment of breast, and stroke her good leg to utter distraction.

We had only two or three dates, given Jeanie's infrequent visits to her uncle's home, but they were dates—my first real ones—and I felt like I was becoming part of the mainstream of teenage life, so unlike my status back in Texas. I was eternally grateful at the time to Jeanie B of Havre de Grace, Maryland, for making that happen, and I still am, as self-condemning of my calculated plan to take advantage as I have learned to be since then.

When I mentioned to my cousin ten or so years later that I had learned to feel guilty for those episodes of delirious making out with a crippled girl, he put one question to me.

"Didn't she like it?"

"I guess so," I said to Addison. "She wrote letters to me after I got back home to Texas."

"There's the answer then," Addison said. "She got something out of it she liked. What did you say when you wrote back to her?"

"I forget," I lied, unable to admit I never answered any of her letters. That was the worst thing I did to Jeanie B, I knew, not the fondling of the parts of her body that were not affected by disease, the parts I wanted to touch, but the refusal to contact her through words on a page. Not to acknowledge her in words, that was true cruelty.

I told her a joke once when she was hanging around the Round Stand where I was working. I did it because it was considered risqué and I wanted to talk sexy to her. I was a man of the world to her, we shared an intimate past, and I wanted to let her know I was a sexual sophisticate.

"Do you know why the guy liked to go boating, Jeanie?" I said as she sipped at the Coke she had bought to give her an excuse to talk to me.

"No, tell me."

"Because he wanted to spend the night on Veronica Lake," I said, waiting for at least a mildly shocked response.

"You know what I want to do, Gerald?" Jeanie B asked.

"What?"

"I want to spend the night under Duff Mountain."

I went off to wait on another customer, completely flummoxed and out of my depth, miscalculating again what a female might do or say. I had treated Jeanie B in a way which made her want me, and I had never intended for that or for anything to happen that wasn't directed completely at me. Things got mixed up, and what I thought I could get done alone I discovered I could not. Other people thought of themselves first, too, even crippled girls who happened to be beautiful. It was more than I was capable of thinking about. I wasn't ready to judge myself, and I knew I'd never fully reach that point.

When I didn't answer Jeanie's letters to me, I did that not to reject her but to quell that part of me which would make me feel worse. I was on the edge of condemning myself, and I couldn't allow that to happen. I had the rest of my life to do that.

CHAPTER 18

Burning the Sofa My Sister Slept On

At the end of each summer spent at Marshall Hall, I came back home to Texas, resumed my role in the family, went back to school, and in all visible respects was not changed a hair in behavior or character. I was still what I was, and I knew where I properly and duly ranked in the social scheme of my life inside and outside of the high school. No dramatic departures from the usual ever occurred. The changes made by my time in Maryland were not recognized by me then, for they were internal and hidden from the world and my consciousness.

I still wanted to be like all those around me; I still was not. I knew I never would feel at home where I had never felt at home before. I talked to people in Polk County about what I'd seen and what I'd done. I bragged about dating Yankee girls, going to Washington, DC, seeing Ted Williams play baseball against the Washington Senators, and did all I could to present myself as a seasoned and sophisticated traveler. I told about drinking beer and parking with girls in my cousin's English car. I wore to school the clothes and suede shoes I had bought in Maryland with money I had made while I lived in a 300-year-old mansion.

No one wanted to hear those stories, driving me by their indifference to spin greater and grander lies. Those I told the lies to and I myself knew that what really mattered was not what happened anywhere outside Livingston High School and Polk County, Texas. We knew where we lived, and we agreed without having to say a word about it that I was still the skinny boy who read all the time, couldn't play any kind of ball, and had no claim in the sexual hierarchy that ruled the day.

I did my best, though, to convince all who would give me attention that I was one of them, and one incident illustrating the failure of that ongoing campaign came when in an eleventh-grade English class one day the teacher asked all of us what we intended to do upon graduation in a year or so. When my turn came to testify, the teacher prefaced her question to me by saying, "I expect Gerald will be way up there in Maryland going to college when the time comes."

I protested that vigorously, saying I would be a college student at Texas A&M, the dream of every male in that part of Texas in those days, and one which probably still lives today. My classmates hooted that down until Mrs. Peace made them hush, and I shrank back behind my desk, knowing that I would never be able to go to A&M, much less any college outside the state of Texas.

But a big change was coming, even as I listened to my classmates remind me of who I truly was, no matter how I lied about it. In 1956, late in the summer just after I returned home from another sentence in the Round Stand at Marshall Hall, my father found a job back in Nederland, the Eden from which we had fallen into East Texas those years before.

We would leave the three-room house with no plumbing in the piney woods near Camp Ruby and the Baptist Church and Estoll Collins's country store, and we would do so without informing Carl Vinson, from whom we rented our home. But we would leave, we would *leave, and* I knew I'd be leaving for good and not come back.

The physical distance between the Old South cotton culture of Polk County and the petro-chemical Gulf Coast plain of Jefferson County is only a little over seventy miles, but the psychic change that my sister Nancy and I felt as we rode in the bed of the truck carrying all our worldly goods toward our once and future home in Nederland was immense. Our parents and our sister rode in the cab with the driver, and Nancy and I were so agreeably stunned to be leaving the smothering pine barrens of East Texas that we rode without a murmur of protest among the bedsteads and mattresses and boxes and chests of drawers open to the view of anyone who might want to see us.

The sofa on which Nancy had slept for several years in the front room of the house on FM Road 1276 did not accompany us with the rest of our goods in the truck. It had made it as far as the front yard, where it was intended for loading into the open truck bed at some point, but I had not been able to bear thinking of its going along with us to the Golden Triangle of Texas. So I put a match to it, and in a matter of minutes it burned away to the metal springs, bolts, and screws which held it together. The fabric and frame were ash.

No one protested what I had done, not even my mother, who invariably saved everything that came into her possession: boxes of jelly glasses, a broken sewing machine, a no-longer-functioning wringer washer, sacks of old clothes, any removeable buttons from shirts and pants that no longer fit, any item that might be salvaged for possible later use. Instead, she observed her older daughter's piece of furniture for sleeping flare up and collapse into embers with a look of calm satisfaction and approval. It smoldered in the yard as we pulled away in the truck, and I watched the smoke rise from it until the place where we had lived for those years was completely out of view.

I didn't return to Carl Vinson's rent house until twenty-two years later when I was attending a summer seminar at Rice University in Houston as representative of Kenyon College in Ohio where I was then chairman of the English department. One Saturday, I took it into my head not to visit an art museum with the other seminarians but to return to the place where my family had left deep East Texas for the Gulf Coast those years ago.

Arriving there and seeing that the house was vacant, I drove my rental car up into the yard where Nancy and I used to ride our cousin Clifford's discarded bicycle around in circles for hours, and parked the car near the porch. Growing from the sandy ground next to the front door was a volunteer scrub pine, which no one had bothered to remove until the sapling was too big to pull up. It was clear that there had been no inhabitants in the place for years.

There was no longer a door to open, and when I stepped into the front room I began reading what random dopers seeking solitude had written on the walls and ceiling. "Welcome to the haunted hut;" and above a well-drawn sketch of a marijuana sprig, "Here's the fun fern." "Fuck me until I faint." "Hook 'em, Horns."

There was no furniture, no longer a woodstove in the front room, nor one for cooking in the kitchen area, no shelf for a water bucket and a wash basin, no sign of where our chifforobe had stood or the chest of drawers, nor any of the beds where we had slept and dreamed our desperation.

I tried to feel something other than the intense need to get back on the road and head for Houston and Rice University, but no specific memory came to mind, no words to sum up, no curses to deliver, no tears to shed. I thought of speaking aloud, alone as I was in the three rooms with none to hear me, of saying something in love and memory to my mother, dead since 1961, or of encouragement and promise to that young self that had lived at one time in that place. "Gerald," I began, but nothing other than my name became available to me, so I said that name again and again until it sounded as strange as a word in a language I had never heard spoken before.

I was not there for me to find, and I have never gone back to discover if I may have returned for another moment to that place.

CHAPTER 19

Arriving Late at Nederland High

We moved into an apartment above a Gulf Oil filling station on Twin City Highway, complete with plumbing and a bathroom with a tub and commode, and the family of Big Willie Duff had access for the first time to indoor conveniences. I have a snapshot from that time of me and my mother sitting on the outside stairway which mounted to our apartment. I don't know what camera recorded the moment or who snapped the shutter, but there we sit in the comparatively urban scene of Nederland, Texas, me grinning around a lit cigarillo between my lips and Dorothy Irwin Duff beside me with an expression of deep relief on her face.

My father was an employee of the City of Nederland in the streets department, a member of a work crew that responded to water leaks and repaired chug holes in municipal roads, and a recipient of a paycheck every two weeks. My mother had some resources to use in the household, my sisters and I were about to enroll in the public schools of Nederland, and the world was opening up before me.

When the day came for Nancy and me to walk the six blocks to the high school for registration and the first day of classes, I explained to her that although we knew from reading the local newspaper, the *Mid County Review,* the exact hour set for showing up, we would be late.

"Why?" Nancy said. "Won't we get in trouble for not being there on time?"

"No," I said. "What can they do to us? We'll just say we thought we were supposed to be there at 8:30, not at 8:00, and they'll take care of us in the office."

"But we know better. Why don't we go when it says to in the paper?"

"Think about this," I said. "Suppose we show up before 8:00, like we're supposed to. What are we going to see when we walk up to that new high school with all those steps leading up to the front door?"

"A bunch of kids standing around waiting to get in when the bell rings?"

"Right," I said. "And what are they going to be doing when we come walking up from the street?"

"Oh," Nancy said. "Oh. Looking at us."

"Every one of them," I said. "They'll know we're new."

"They might say something to us," Nancy said.

"And they might not," I said.

I wrote that scene in a novel published forty-five years later, and the character who suffered the inspection by the clots of strange teenagers waiting for the school bell to ring was as humiliated and self-conscious during the experience as I knew my sister and I would have been if we had let ourselves undergo the ordeal. I made my fictional character take the hit we had dodged those years before. He could stand it.

When we arrived a little after 8:30 on that September morning at Nederland High School, the steps were empty, as were the halls, and Nancy and I walked to the office unimpeded, unmolested, and unobserved by our peers. The grumpiness of the office staff at having to deal with late arrivals was of no consequence to us, and Nancy was impressed, though not willing to admit it, with the wisdom of her big brother about the social mores of the adolescent.

"Everybody's already in the auditorium listening to the principal," the office clerk fussed at us. "You're missing all that. Just go to the room assigned you on this information sheet and wait for them to show up."

"Yes, ma'am," I said. "We sure will."

Although I didn't understand the reasons for it at the time, I learned immediately that the people I was going to school with in Nederland were different in a profound way from my classmates in East Texas. It wasn't just the way they dressed, though that was a part of it. The boys all wore T-shirts, blue jeans, and footwear that could be classified as moccasins, though the shoes were never called that. No one ever talked about what they wore, and hardly ever mentioned clothes, either in praise or ridicule.

The girls wore skirts and blouses, sometimes pedal-pushers and capri pants, and the only individualizing adornments were colored and patterned scarves knotted about their necks. The ones romantically attached wore senior rings on chains or sometimes on their fingers, appropriately wound with tape to make them secure enough to stay on.

The Nederland Bulldogs were a football power in the state, and lots of black and gold letter jackets were in evidence but only on pep rally days and typically only on girlfriends of players. The players themselves, even the ones who were all-state or all-district as attested by sleeve patches, hardly ever wore their trophy clothing to school.

No one seemed interested in what anybody's father did for a living, and the sons and daughters of doctors and lawyers and businessmen were not singled out for regular identification by the social status of their families, as was always the case in Polk County in deep East Texas.

It wasn't until years later when I was first trying to write fiction that I made myself think in detail about the reasons for these differences. At the time I was a student in Nederland, I was deeply satisfied not to have to apologize over and over for my family background and my father's occupation, and not having to brood over the status that accorded me was a blessing and a deep breath of fresh air.

What it all meant demographically was that East Texas was Old South and the Gulf Coast was petro-chemical. Where you fit in the infinitely fine gradations of class in East Texas mattered, and it mattered strongly in the pine barrens of a vanished plantation culture. Which oil or chemical company paid your daddy's hourly wage in the Golden Triangle of Texas was of little consequence. A great leveling had been accomplished and was firmly in place, and other ways to distinguish quality and worth operated in Nederland and the similar communities surrounding the city.

I was invited to the homes of classmates in Nederland in a way I never was in Livingston, and I frequently discovered large differences in the financial resources of the families of my friends. But that couldn't be detected by observing them in the halls and parking lots and classrooms of Nederland High School. They all looked alike, dressed alike, and walked alike. Many drove cars to school, and for those who smoked, an area outside a side entrance to the high school building was set aside for lighting up and puffing away.

By the time students had achieved senior status, the usual topic of discussion in the smoking area was who had and who hadn't gone across the river during the past weekend and who planned to do so the next time Friday and Saturday arrived. The river was the Sabine, which marks the boundary between Texas and Louisiana, and it was just a little over twenty miles from Nederland. Lined up just over the state line in Louisiana were the honky-tonks which called to all who had transportation and a few dollars to spend on cover charges, and the beer and liquor available to anybody ready to buy.

Lou Ann's and the Big Oak Club were the main attractions, nobody got carded in Southwest Louisiana, and everybody who could ask for a drink could buy one. The music was a combination of blues, country, swamp rock, and zydeco, and it drew people from everywhere in the Golden Triangle, including those later to make their own mark in the trade. Edgar and Johnny Winter, Jimmy Clanton, the Big Bopper, Johnny Preston, and destined to be the most famous of all, Janis Joplin from Thomas Jefferson High in Port Arthur. Black bands like Cookie and the Cupcakes, Clifton Chenier, and Classy Ballou were only a few of the many laying down the sounds that accompanied us as we drank across the river.

Back at Nederland High during the school week, different degrees of merit were assigned to all inhabitants, but the gradations of what constituted the acceptable, the outstanding, and the untouchable were not marked by the badges I had observed in the pine barrens of Polk County. Many more niches of classification were allowed in the youth culture of the Gulf Coast, and the things that mattered were much more varied.

Sitting to my left in senior English class were Wallace Kay and Margaret Leyseth. He was an academically ambitious student with one of the highest grade averages in the class of 1957, and that fact made him eligible to go steady with Margaret, a head majorette in the marching band and therefore a prize. Vying with Wallace in the race for valedictorian status was Cole Williams, who was also an all-state running back for the Bulldogs. But Cole's football player role didn't seem to give him any advantage over Wallace that I could determine, an amazing departure from what I had observed in Polk County.

I soon established my own credentials as a grade grubber and was given approval and recognition for that fact, not only by the teachers but by my senior classmates. That didn't make sense, given the medieval world view I had learned in my bones in East Texas, but I seized upon the new reality.

The teachers in the public schools of that era in American education were almost all women, and there was an immutable reason for that. The only employment opportunities for intelligent educated females in that age were nursing and teaching, which meant that the women who taught us were typically sane, intellectually confident, and personally tough-minded. They expected us to learn, whether we were capable of doing so or willing to do so, and they cut us very little slack. They were glad to have jobs that allowed them to exercise their wits and ambition, and students and public education profited from those sociological and economic conditions which repressed women otherwise.

The fact that being female is today no longer the bar to advancement and choice and opportunity that it was then has been disastrous for public education, beneficial though it has been to millions of individual women. In the 1950s, the male teachers I encountered in my public school education were for the most part coaches of various athletic teams who had to teach in order to make a living in the world of the bottom-feeders.

My world history teacher at Nederland High School had been a quarterback at Texas A&M on a Bear Bryant team. He was at Nederland because of the fame of its football program, marking time until he could advance to the next level of coaching, and he was as unqualified to teach as I was to play football. His name was Elwood Kettler, and he has since become recognized as a famous member of the Junction Boys that Bear Bryant made into a championship team at A&M before he went to his final apotheosis at Alabama.

Kettler would read to us out of the textbook, snarl at any sign of life in the classroom, and intimidate us into dead silence by his demeanor and well-demonstrated contempt for what he was being forced to do to make a living as he waited for deliverance from being indoors. He did name me as winner of the medal for best student of world history, however, and I kept that memento in my wallet until I lost it years later when I was in graduate school.

CHAPTER 20

The Way Louisiana Girls Smelled

My best friend in my single year at Nederland High School was Wayland Austin, who dyed his blonde hair black to be different, and who became a favorite of my mother because of his manners and charm. Once when he had come by to pick me up in his '50 Ford, she asked me why I also insisted in going places with Pete Hardy, another classmate not nearly so pleasing to mothers as Wayland.

"I don't like that Pete Hardy," she said. "He always looks like he's up to something. Wayland is who you ought to spend time with."

She was right. Pete looked like he was up to something because he certainly wanted to be but was never able to get up to the level required for dissipation. Wayland Austin, an accomplished conversationalist with older women, looked the part of a steady reliable boy, ever ready for a polite joke and a laugh, and he was all that. But he also was the one who introduced me to life across the river, to deeper acquaintance with alcohol and tobacco, and to girls ready to date a skinny boy heretofore accustomed mainly to reading books and lying about what he hadn't done yet and wanted desperately to do.

The first time Wayland took me across the Sabine to the sin centers of Cajun Louisiana we pulled into the parking lot of the Big Oak Club well after dark. When we got out of the car, we could hear the blast of guitars, drums, and saxophones coming from the band and cutting through the mist and Spanish moss hanging in the trees. It was Jay Richard and the Blues Kings doing a cover of Jimmy Reed's "Honest I Do," and it seemed to lift us off the gravel of the parking lot and float us into the building.

Inside, we ordered drinks, kept our eyes averted from those of any males milling about, and scanned the crowd for signs of females willing to dance. "Don't tell anybody we're from Texas," Wayland warned me. "These Louisiana guys don't like Texans worth a damn. They will kick your ass."

"What if somebody asks me where I'm from?" I said.

"Lie," Wayland said. "Tell them you're from Lake Charles or Sulphur. Say you working on an oil rig. Act like you're not still in school."

That was easier said than done, but I flung in and tried every time anybody spoke to me, which was seldom. The girls I approached for dancing had nothing to say, either taking the hand I extended and joining me on the dance floor or refusing to acknowledge the offering to join me in a clinch dance by simply looking away when I walked up to where they were.

The first thing I noticed when one accepted the gambit was the overwhelmingly different way Louisiana females smelled as compared to the girls I had sneaked off from home to dance with before in Texas at the Catholic recreation hall in Nederland on Friday nights. This new smell wasn't unpleasant, but it was deeper and less perfumed than that from the high school sophomores I picked out for approach at home. The hair of the Louisiana girls was damp with sweat from dancing in the heat and humidity of the unairconditioned Big Oak Club, they pushed their faces right into the space between my cheek and my neck, and they had little or nothing to say. They weren't there to become my friend or romantic interest. They wanted to dance, they wanted to drink, they wanted to smoke filter-tipped cigarettes, and they wanted to do all that with somebody who acted like he knew what he was doing.

I was out of my league, and I knew it. But I didn't let that bother me, satisfied to the core that some of them would let me hold them tight, stumble about the dance floor, and smell that musky scent arising from Louisiana girls. It was hot, I was sweating, the music was so loud I couldn't hear my own voice when I tried to make small talk, but I could feel myself becoming by the minute—there in a honky-tonk across the river—less of a reader of books and more of a male animal in the hunt.

I would have something to lie about back in school on Monday, and that I did.

CHAPTER 21

Margaret, I Could Have Been a Good Abe Lincoln for You

Somewhere along in the middle of the school year, try-outs were announced for would-be actors in the senior class play. Something compelled me to give it a shot, probably my uncertain sense of who I was, wanted to be, or would be, and I showed up at the appointed time. I got a part, a small one certainly, but it had a couple of speaking lines. I was satisfied to consider myself now part of the theater, able to go to rehearsals, hang around backstage, swap what we thespians considered clever and cutting remarks, and watch Margaret Leyseth pledge her love as Mary Todd to Lester Moye as a gawky young Prairie Lawyer in rut.

The play chosen by our teacher/director to be presented by the senior class that year was the hideously awful adaptation from the more hideously awful Irving Stone novel *Love Is Eternal*, depicting the developing love affair between Abe Lincoln, the fated-to-be savior of his nation, and Mary Todd, the southern belle from Lexington, Kentucky, set in the town of Springfield, Illinois. We believed we were involved in presenting one of the most serious and important dramas of the Western world, since Miss Adele Forest told us that at each rehearsal, and we did our best to recognize and represent the aura of the impending Civil War and Lincoln's assassination in Ford's Theatre hanging over our brave efforts to interpret young love between historically significant people.

We tried, I swear we did, or at least Margaret Leyseth, Lester Moye, and myself as Reverend Draper, the young couple's spiritual mentor and guide, did as we hammered away at learning lines and remembering in which order they came. I knew I was much more suited in my soul to portray deep moral, intellectual, and historical truths than was Lester Moye—and to look down Margaret Leyseth's low-cut costume in the process—but I did have the problem of stuttering like a sewing machine gone berserk and of delivering my lines at a speed calculated to get through the entire two-hour production in about twenty minutes if my rate of speech were maintained by all the other players.

So instead I mooned about the backstage, sneaking cigarettes and repeating my two lines over and over again so as not to forget them before the curtain rose at the magic time of opening night. I can still say one of them, delivered when someone asked where young Abe had gotten off to on the first occasion of the public announcement of his betrothal to the vixen from Kentucky. "He mentioned something about Urbana," I was to deliver, and years later when I drove my 1956 Chevrolet past the city limits sign of the location of the University of Illinois where I was to begin work for the doctorate, I said them aloud again with proper enunciation and force.

The best thing about being in the senior play was the fact that I had to have my hair, then black and abundant, temporarily colored gray on the nights of the production. To avoid having to redo the 'do, I went to my daytime high school classes resplendent in my gray hair, and all who saw me had to know I was an actor, in between shows, and that my true self was in waiting for an audience.

I used my experience in the 1957 senior class play in my novel *Coasters* published over forty years later, hoping that reviewers would comment on the hilarity and genius of that section of my fictive account in particular, but none ever did.

But at the time, I wasn't just Gerald Duff, all 145 pounds of him, but an actor occupying another sensibility, weary of the quotidian and able to brighten and enlighten the insular worlds of those hungry for the glamour of drama. We even had a late-night cast party after the last production, held in a seafood restaurant in Bridge City, on the banks of the Neches River, complete with Johnny Youngblood's smuggling in a bottle of vodka for us to spike the lemonade.

I might not have been able to make any athletic team or drive a nice car, but I could put on a costume, dye my hair, deliver lines before an audience, and drink spiked lemonade until the car lights on the Rainbow Bridge over the Neches River (the highest bridge in the state of Texas at that time) swam before my jaded thespian eyes. Oh, Margaret, I could have been such a good Abe for you!

Graduation from Nederland High School took place the evening of May 27, 1957, in the school auditorium, and I marched in the procession, attired in cap and gown, feeling the full weight and ceremonial significance of the moment. Nobody else in the senior class did, I was to learn later from my sister Nancy.

"You were the only one who acted funny," she told me. "Everybody else just walked down the aisle like a regular person, but you took weird steps as you walked, like you were trying to get over something lying on the floor in front of you."

I dismissed what she said with fiery contempt, but I was worried that maybe others had the same interpretation of my solemn gait as she had described. All I was trying to do, I knew in my bones, was to treat the moment with the seriousness it deserved, and I was damned if I was going to slouch along looking from side to side for friends and family members in the audience like all the C students were doing. I was graduating, and I would be going to college, maybe to Texas A&M if that scholarship deal came through. I had to act like I was in the middle of a big moment, and I did.

CHAPTER 22

Multiple Choice Questions

The possibility of having a free ride at A&M had been communicated to me several months before graduation day by the school counselor, Mr. Rodney Branch, known popularly as Mr. Rod, a label he demanded that we students use when we spoke of him. When he called me in out of homeroom one morning in early spring, he had said there was a scholarship competition at Texas A&M open to a single candidate from each high school in Texas. Nederland High would be pleased to nominate me to take the battery of written tests in College Station if I proved myself eligible.

But before Mr. Rod told me that, he chose from his repertoire of war stories a suitable one to relate to me, as he always did in every counseling session with any student. The one about the foxhole, though, not his whole series.

"Son," he said, "before we get started on what opportunity I want to talk to you about, let me tell you something that happened to me. I think it'll speak volumes and tell you something you ought to remember for the rest of your life."

I looked eager and attentive, and I was that, having come to the conclusion by that point in life that I should always defer to authority figures, listen to what they had to say, and try to profit from their wisdom. I believed their motives were good, they were interested in my welfare, and they intended nothing but to advance me. They wanted to help. I was probably the only member of the Nederland senior class still of that persuasion.

"I was lying in the mud and blood of a foxhole in Belgium, Gerald," Mr. Rod said. "It was during the Battle of the Bulge, and I was hanging on with the rest of my buddies to stay alive and beat the Germans. You know what the Battle of the Bulge was, don't you?"

"Yessir," I said. "My father has talked to me about it."

"Was your dad there?" Mr. Rod said, rousing himself in his office chair and looking up from the pencil he liked to use as a pointer at crucial moments in a counseling session.

"No sir," I said. "He was in the Pacific Theater of the war." I was lying, of course, since my father was forty-two years old when the war began and never served a day in the military, but I figured the more rapport I could establish with Mr. Rod the more good it might do me. I knew he'd never meet my father to check my story, since Mr. Rod had gone to college, and to my knowledge my father had never met anyone who had done that except some of his nieces who were teachers in East Texas.

"He had it bad, too, then, but it wasn't the Bulge," Mr. Rod allowed. "But I was there in the foxhole, and it came to me as I listened to the German 88 shells flying over my head and killing our boys what I wanted to do if I survived. You know what that was?"

I did, of course, having been told by many other seniors what it was that Mr. Rod had realized as his life's goal in that foxhole. But I told him I had no idea.

"To help kids," he said. "That's what came to me that I wanted to do."

Mr. Rod teared up briefly at that point, his voice wavering a bit as he remembered his epiphany in the mudhole in Belgium, and then he went manfully on. "Kids like you is what I'm talking about. 'Just let me live and get back home,' I told the Lord, 'and I'll dedicate my life to the young people of Texas. I'll carry out that part of the bargain, if You'll carry out Yours.'"

I nodded, my face carefully composed into a mask of strength, appreciation, and sorrow at what Mr. Rod had promised the Lord to do and maybe, just maybe, would do some of for me.

"First of all, Gerald," he said. "We got to see if you're eligible and can show need. What does your dad do for a living?"

"He is a common laborer," I said, the phrase popping into my head as a good substitute for what I didn't really want to admit in detail: my father worked for Streets and Alleys for the City of Nederland, digging ditches, patching holes and loading garbage. "That's all he is."

Mr. Rod looked astonished at what I'd just said, and I realized the phrase I'd used had earned me the right to receive the endorsement of Nederland High School to go to College Station, take a bunch of tests, and maybe get to go free to Texas A&M. The way you said something, the words you chose to cast your thoughts in, the slant that language could put on reality, all this could help you along the way. I already knew how to lie directly about what and who I was, and the success of my calling my father a *common laborer*, a term I had never heard anybody use to describe an occupational status before, said I didn't have to make things up out of whole cloth, necessarily. A little slant would do. Call something by the right name, and people might do something for you. What you named a thing could give you an advantage over other people, even if you had to shame yourself.

So one Saturday morning I got to go to College Station to face that test that stood between me and a free ride at Texas A&M. It was my one chance at becoming an Aggie.

My family still didn't have a car, so we all loaded into Bill Commolander's Ford sedan, all of us except for my sister Nancy who was allowed to stay behind at a girlfriend's house. My father, mother, little sister, and I, with City of Nederland Streets and Alleys worker Bill Commolander driving his car and lighting Camels one off the other, took off early for the trip. To my parents and little sister, to be able to travel that far in an automobile was a treat, and to me it was a journey akin to what gladiators underwent as they prepared to emerge from their underground chambers into the blinding light of the coliseum of Rome.

The buildings of Texas A&M were gray and many. The room in which we hundreds of aspiring Aggies underwent examination was monstrous, and I made my fatal mistake immediately when I responded to the first question asking what I intended as a major if I were to be admitted to the all-male bastion of A&M. *Petroleum engineering*, I carefully wrote in the slot provided, following the universal advice given all students in Texas intending college study. That was where the jobs and the money were, all citizens of the Lone Star State knew, and I intended to be as much like everybody else as I possibly could. I had spent my life so far in that quest, and I wasn't about to quit. Yet.

I would be an engineer. I would work in the petro-chemical industry of Texas. I would be a man among men and a Texan among Texans.

So as I answered the questions put to me on the Texas A&M examination, I knew that the easy ones, the ones about what one word is to another word as a specified word is to another, were not really important. And reading short paragraphs to pick out thesis statements was also so simple as to be beneath contempt. What mattered were all the stated problems about mathematical situations and gas density changes and predictions of appropriate next numbers in a given sequence of other numbers. Those were the traps set to trip me up and keep me from a free education into how to be a petroleum engineer and an Aggie. At least the questions were multiple choice.

It wasn't until several months later while I was working my last summer in the Round Stand at Marshall Hall Amusement Park in Maryland that I received a letter from my mother letting me know I wouldn't be going to A&M and to glory after all. "I've applied for you at Lamar," she wrote, "and you'll be registering for classes right after Labor Day. I'm sorry you didn't get into A&M, but it's probably for the best. It's a long way from Nederland to College Station. You need to get you a smallpox shot before Lamar will let you in."

I got the smallpox shot, and my arm swelled and festered and burned all the way to Texas as I rode the bus back south. I bought and smoked several packs of cigarettes, Kent filters—since I liked the way the package looked—all the way home, looking out the window in jaded and bitter resignation. I would not be an Aggie, but a commuter student at Lamar State College of Technology in Beaumont, eight miles from Nederland.

CHAPTER 23

A Need for Relief

LAMAR'S MASCOT WAS A BIRD, THE CARDINAL, AND THE COLLEGE WAS CALLED, by the young of the Golden Triangle doomed to attend it, Tweety Bird High and Pecker Tech, and any other names we could come up with to demonstrate our understanding of our situation and where we truly were. We knew we had to do that before anyone else explained it to us.

When I arrived at Lamar in 1957 and began to attend my classes in physics, chemistry, calculus, dynamics, statics, strength of materials, I discovered to my dismay that the constructors of the examinations at Tweety Bird High were as interested in the arcane and the abstruse and the quantitative as the ones who had built the tests that stopped me from going to Texas A&M on a free ride. It was hard. It wasn't interesting, and the courses that I had to take in general education proved to be as easy as the ones I had aced in high school. I made As in English and history and political science, but I struggled to get Cs in the courses taken by serious students of engineering, those who would go on to real jobs in the petro-chemical industry in Beaumont and Houston and New Orleans.

I was ashamed of myself as a student for the first time. Not only did I not rank in the top group in my classes, I dwelled with the ordinary, the slow, the confused, the witless. And the As I made were in female-dominated subjects. I could read the poems and stories assigned in my English courses with greater understanding than anyone around me, but I kept quiet about that, instead bemoaning falsely with my fellow engineering students the difficulty of writing assignments.

I found I had to lie in a new way, downplaying my successes and inflating my weaknesses. It made for headaches and confusion. When my mother would ask me what grades I was making, I lied by citing only my high marks in the liberal arts courses, those beneath contempt for an engineer, and I concealed the Cs and occasional Ds on work in the *real* courses, those that could result in an actual job with real pay.

I avoided all mirrors in my first two years at Pecker Tech, and I found more need to make things up than I ever had before, even in East Texas. Life was supposed to get easier, but it hadn't. I was still an accomplished and adept liar, but I was feeling the strain.

I did get to date girls at Lamar, though, since so many of them had never known me in high school and consequently didn't realize my true ranking as an impossible sexual partner. In a short story I wrote years later, I had a female character, drunk and miserable with her weakly inept husband, advise another woman. "Don't never," she says, "date outside your high school. You'll never understand what a slack-twisted, French Club-going, Student Council-representing drip you're about to hook up with unless you've had the chance to see him in high school. They can't lie to you if you knew them then."

The girls in my classes at Lamar looked like grown women to me, dressed in their penny loafers and plaid skirts and white blouses adorned with circle pins, with their hair cut short and maintained by heavy-duty hairspray, and their coolly distant facial expressions. They were daunting, but they were from outside my high school and unfamiliar with the males they were allowing to take them to movies and dances and honky-tonks. They didn't know any better about the nature of the strange males they were dealing with, and I saw no reason to disabuse them of their misconceptions.

Around them and in the hunt, I found new reasons to exaggerate and inflate, to imply a storied past of dissolution and familiarity with the social scene, and to lie baldly and outright when the need arose.

Once when I was invited to a fraternity luau held on McFadden Beach near Galveston, I was forced to come to painful terms with how easy it was for some Lamar females to see all the way through me. I had asked a particular woman to go with me to the event because I had learned she was already divorced, as young as she was, and I was expecting great and good things to result. All of us knew that a woman who had been married and then divorced was accustomed to sexual encounters on a regular and sustained basis.

"Thing of it is," Carl Dameron from Port Arthur once memorably said to a bunch of us as we nursed beers in Salhab's near the campus, "you got to understand that a divorced woman who is used to steady screwing goes kind of nutty when she's cut off from it all of a sudden. She might've learned to hate her sorry husband enough to quit him, but she will miss getting that steady ration of dong."

"Her juices have done been started into flowing," Ray Ener added to Carl's analysis, "so when she's not getting that screwing every night, they get all dammed up. She gets nervous and crazy for somebody to give her what she needs."

"A divorced woman has got to have it," Carl said. "And she is not particular about who she wants to give it to her. She's finished with that romance and flowers shit. That stuff left with the guy she split the sheets with. Now she just wants the prod."

That appealed to all of us there in Salhab's. We knew we didn't give a damn about that romance and flowers shit ourselves, certainly not enough to admit it publicly, and what Carl and Ray had explained to us about the effect of custom, the damming up of female secretions, and the subsequent overwhelming need among divorced women for relief from such situations made perfect sense. We knew how we'd feel if we ever got a chance for steady screwing, as Carl put it so succinctly, and had it snatched away from us by a divorce decree.

When Frank Sturrock told me he could fix me up with a divorced woman, now a student at Lamar whom he had known in Silsbee High School, I knew that would give me my best chance yet. I hoped I would be up to the task of satisfying her pent-up passions as the dam holding back her juices broke under my approach, but I was willing to do my best to give her what she needed. So I jumped at the chance to ask Maude Gwinnett to accompany me to the APO luau. I was not fearful of sexual dysfunction, never having heard of the concept, and I figured I could bluff my way through anything once. I knew the lying game backwards and forwards. She would believe I knew the ropes.

I called the number Frank Sturrock had given me for the divorced woman, and she answered on the first ring, confirming the truths about females in her situation, as I saw it. She's been sitting by the phone, I thought, hoping some man would want to get with her, and luckily I caught her at home before somebody else offered her relief today.

When I told her who I was and mentioned Frank, she didn't say anything immediately, and then spoke. "Oh, yeah. I remember a Frank," she said. "He was in the band. Played one of those big horns. What's it called?"

"A trumpet?"

"That's not big," Maude Gwinnett said, familiar, I assumed, with the size of all kinds of things. "A trombone. You got a class with him, huh?"

"Strength of materials," I said in what I meant as a familiar and somewhat bored tone. "I'm an engineer."

She agreed to go to the luau with me, on the strength of the materials I had presented, I surmised, and because she was feeling the terrible pressures of sexual deprivation. That notion hovered in my mind as she rode along beside me the following Saturday on the way to McFadden Beach, Bob Thurman and his girlfriend in the backseat of the Chevrolet alternately sucking at cans of Schlitz and each other's faces on the way to the luau.

Maude didn't say much, and I said less, struck dumb by what was happening in the backseat between Bob and his steady and by trying to guess what was roaring through the divorced woman's brain as we worked our way toward the Gulf, and what I hoped would happen once we arrived. I was prepared to be patient. There would have to be a period of drinking, building a bonfire, roasting wienies, splashing in the waves, screaming and laughing, all to the sounds of radios in the cars tuned to the Les Ledet and Gordon Baxter rock and roll program on KPAC, before the sun went down enough for people to start pairing off for the real business of the luau.

She was likely aching for that to take place, I considered, desperate as she had to be for what a divorced woman was used to and wasn't getting any more, and that hovering desire likely accounted for her silence as we worked our way toward the water.

Once there, after a decent period of socializing and jabbering with other partiers, I managed to get Maude Gwinnett off to the side and seated on a blanket, cans of beer stuck in the sand next to us, and the sun hanging on the horizon as the sounds of luau thundered about us.

"How long did you and your husband stay married?" I asked, figuring to ease into an implied consideration of what happened constantly in the life together of a legally wed couple. Get her to thinking about what she's not getting on a regular basis these days, I told myself, and see if those dammed up juices would begin to rumble and seep.

"Way too long," Maude said. "This beer is hot. Why don't they have a keg at this party? Paper cups keep it cool longer than old cans."

"I'll be glad to look for you a paper cup," I told her gallantly. "I saw some girls with some a while ago."

"That's all right," she said. "Just relax. I can get along without it."

She hadn't really looked at me yet for longer than a couple of seconds at a time, probably a little shy and nervous being this close to a man and what he could do for her in her current state of sexual starvation, I considered. She was probably uncertain about how much interest she should be showing at this early stage of our relationship, accustomed as she was to stripping off her clothes and getting down to business in short order whenever she was alone with a man. She didn't know how to act with this college crowd at a luau.

"What was your husband's name?" I asked, determined to make her get her mind off beer and focus on the business at hand. The sun was still nailed to the horizon of the Gulf as though it had forgotten how to get out of town and let the dark take over. It was time for things to move along.

"The same as it is now. Why do you want to know?"

"Maybe I met him before," I said. "I don't know. What kind of job has he got? Did he do shift work? Did he work nights?"

"He worked nights every chance he got," Maude said, taking a hit off her can of warm beer. "Ronald Gene is a cop in Silsbee, and he stayed out at night as much as he could every night that rolled."

"His name is Ronald Gene?" I said, imagining a jealous cop coming after anybody daring to date the woman he was divorced from. He'd be big, muscled up, and used to knocking people around.

"Yeah, but I didn't call him that."

"You didn't?"

"No, I called him *Shithead* and *Asshole*, mainly. Sometimes I called him worse than that."

Maude was wearing a modest swim suit, with a flowered shirt layered over it, an attempt at a luau motif, and I noticed that, although her legs from the knees down were smoothly slick, that she had not shaved her thighs. A good measure of black hairs longer and more pronounced than any I could boast were sprinkled on her legs all the way up to the skirt-like arrangement of her swimsuit. I couldn't keep from staring.

"You didn't like your husband?" I said to the black thigh hairs.

"No. I got sick to death of him," Maude said. "Now let me ask you something, for a change."

"What's that?" I said, thinking that now she's about to get down to business.

"You haven't dated much, have you?" she said in what I could tell she meant to be a kind tone. That was the worst thing about her question. She didn't want to hurt my feelings.

I was so taken aback by that observation that I lifted my gaze from Maude's leg hairs to look her directly in the eyes as I started to explain to her in great detail and with persuasive force my long history of successful dating. I did well enough at that to win the argument, I knew, since she stopped talking and said she felt like walking down the beach by herself for a while, but I never got to touch Maude that night and I never saw her again. I suspected she went back to Silsbee and found somebody more to her liking, somebody less collegiate and intellectual than I was.

When I was asked later by Carl and Ray and the others who were waiting on the news about how my beach date with a divorced woman had gone, I just smiled, said I was too tired to talk about it, and spoke in confirmation of the current theory about the desperate needs of divorced women.

"I bet she got there before you did," Carl said, "crazy as she was for it."

"Let's just say it wasn't even close," I said, coolly puffing at my Kent cigarette and smiling like Jay Gatsby deep in a memory of Daisy.

It was not long after that well-deserved humiliation at the beach that I underwent a further and total shattering of my misconceptions about what goes on between men and women. What I thought was true was all wrong. Again. I didn't end up like Jay Gatsby, in a swimming pool dead from faulty illusions, but I did have my utterly wrong notions about the true nature of the relationship between the sexes reformed for good. I came to realize that I knew as little about that overwhelmingly fascinating topic as I did about electrical engineering.

Real women taught me that lesson, and it was one I had to learn the hard way: by dint of experience, trial and error, and admission of fault.

CHAPTER 24

A Change of Major

THE BREAKING POINT IN MY ACADEMIC CAREER AS A STUDENT IN THE COLLEGE of engineering at Lamar State College of Technology came in the first semester of my junior year. I had passed enough math, physics, chemistry, and introductory engineering courses to be required to take my first serious class in electrical engineering, or *Double E* as it was called among the cognoscenti. It was taught by a young man named Carlin, who wore bowties, a burr haircut, and a perpetually eager look as he raced through explanations of circuits and set us problems in determining the numerical value of various functions key to electrical phenomena.

I didn't know what the fuck he was talking about, and neither did my lab partner, Warren Murphy, also from Nederland and about whom I would write a novel, *Coasters,* forty years later. We both hated and despised Carlin, in particular the way he expressed amazement at our stupidity in all things Double E and his eagerness to work with us individually to bring us along in the study of his insane and passionate obsession.

"Carlin can kiss my ass," Warren said once as we sat in the Student Union brooding over topics electrical. "The way he's always trying to make me understand that shit and work those problems. I hope the fuckers never get worked. Figure the electrical flux about a given point, bullshit."

"He's got a nerve, all right," I said. "Thinking I can learn that stuff."

"Or want to," Warren said.

That was the breakthrough for me, Warren's voicing what I knew to the core was the truth about me and engineering, about me and the real world of practical problems and their solution, about me and preparation for a job that paid good money and would get me located forever in the Golden Triangle of Texas, the heart of the petro-chemical industry of the Gulf Coast.

I didn't want to deal with real things. I wanted to read poems and stories that made no difference in the sensible world of work and practicality. I wanted to worry about why words were arranged in a certain fashion to achieve a certain effect that made no difference to anybody and caused nothing to happen. I wanted to make a professional study and a lifelong commitment to lies, their creation, the needless telling of them, and to marveling over their beauty. I wanted to devote myself to the useless and the impractical. What better way to do that at a college of technology than to change my major to English?

So that same afternoon, I knocked on the door of my academic advisor, whose contempt for me as a student of electrical engineering was justifiably palpable and ongoing, and informed him I was taking a new direction as far as the college of engineering was concerned. My foot's in the stirrup, my pony can't stand; goodbye, old partner, I'm leaving Cheyenne.

"Well, Mr. Duff," Dr. Georges Michaelides said in heavily accented English learned somewhere in another country, "not all of us have got the good ability. It's best for you to be whatever this English major is. You'll teach little children how to do the English, right?"

"Right," I told him and left his office to find my slide rule. That instrument was about to get what it deserved.

I had a lot to make up in a short period of time, determined as I was not to spend more than four years in college, so I registered for an overload of courses and set plans for summer school attendance. With much effort over the next few months, I also grew a goatee, not having the ability to cultivate a mustache along with my incompetence in dealing with the material world of engineering, and I bought myself a used set of bongo drums.

Warren Murphy played at a guitar, and he and I joined forces in attempting to write and sing folk songs, despite the fact we couldn't read music and had no talent for performance. But as I tapped away at the bongos in the daytime and read Jack Kerouac's *On the Road* and Allan Ginsburg's *Howl* in the midnight hours, for the first time I was happy to be in college. I accepted that what I liked was worthless, non-profitable in the long and short terms, which at Lamar would get me classified as verging on queer, but I could do it and I could do it well. Comparatively speaking.

I delighted my long-suffering mother by making the dean's list each semester until graduation, I did not inform Big Willie Duff of my change of direction in major and in life, and I found friends among my classmates for the first time since I had walked onto the campus of the Lamar State College of Technology.

Like me, they had no future in the petro-chemical industry, with its offer of gleaming financial rewards and prestige; they didn't wear slide rules strapped to their belts, and they didn't know a thing about electrical flux about a certain point in a circuit, given a specific changing surge in current. They did not deal in certainties. They couldn't nail down the truth of any equation, and they did not profess to understand the physical world of the Golden Triangle of Texas, or of anywhere else.

They wandered about the campus and the one coffee shop available in Beaumont, The Sage, speaking loudly about whatever floated through their non-quantitative minds. They happily and enviously sneered at engineers, and I sank to the nadir of practical ability they represented as though I were falling into a featherbed.

It was around that time that I met the woman who would be my first wife, accompany me to the places of my graduate work, bear my two children, and in her early twenties manifest what a series of psychiatrists defined as schizophrenia. I didn't know any of that was coming, naturally. All I knew was that she had long blonde hair falling to the middle of her back, a pretty face, and an ability to draw and paint pictures.

That satisfied my new understanding of myself down to the ground, and we rushed into marriage. In less than eighteen months after we had met, we had packed our possessions into the bed of the pickup borrowed from her father and left for Fayetteville, Arkansas, where I would begin work toward a master's degree in English. I left behind my mother dying of cancer, my father, and my twelve-year-old sister. I have never forgiven myself for not staying by Dorothy Irwin Duff's side until her death only a few months after that day of departure in late August of 1961.

But I didn't let myself think of her death at the time. I was headed north, and I would study literature and be a college professor. I was the essence of selfishness, as I had always been, and I had no time for anyone else. I would find a way to persuade myself that what I was doing was the right thing to do. I had always done that before, and I could do it again easily. I had made myself a master of mendacity, and I was prepared to lean on the self I had earned.

CHAPTER 25

Licking Down My Lunch in Fayetteville

WHEN I ARRIVED AT FAYETTEVILLE IN AT AGE TWENTY-TWO WITH MY NEW WIFE and some sticks of furniture and a few boxes, for the first time in my life I wasn't living with my parents. I had commuted to Lamar from Nederland, and I had worked at a series of jobs to finance my attempts at achieving a collegiate experience, but I slept every night in the house my father rented. In the late afternoons, I was the janitor at the administration building of the Nederland Independent School District and early in the morning at the Agricultural Stabilization Office in Beaumont. In the summers, I sold *Collier's New Encyclopedias* door to door, and I worked for the J.D. Chester Construction Company, which subcontracted for the Sun Oil Company, the outfit that had fired my father in 1948 and set in operation our exodus to East Texas. I was a TV cameraman at the new ABC affiliate in Beaumont, channel twelve, a non-union concern looking for cheap and untrained labor willing to work for nothing. I was all that, and my first day on the job, I shot the local evening news with the first camera I had ever seen, much less touched.

At all of these jobs, I was not a good employee, terrible in fact except for the camera-man gig, which did engage my interest. It was show business, after all, and the idea of that allowed me to inflate the importance of what I was doing sufficiently to concentrate my attention. I began the janitor's job well, cleaning the assigned areas to a gleaming finish, but that didn't last. I left both janitor jobs one step ahead of being fired.

The job with the construction company taught me the habit of licking down my lunch in view of my fellow workers to keep them from eating my sandwiches and banana cakes when I wasn't looking. "I'm licking it," all of us would announce as we performed that ritual on arrival at the job site before beginning the work of the day. It took only one empty lunch sack to teach me the wisdom of licking everything down so all the world could see. You mark your territory by defiling it.

One of the black coworkers I knew early in my career in construction work voiced the core reason to continue my college education, even though I was offered the chance by my boss of staying on at the end of the summer. The pay was good, the work they gave me to do easy enough. But one morning right before we picked up the tools we would be using in the day, the middle-aged black man whose name was Wendell Washington spoke the words that tipped me back toward reregistration at Lamar, as misplaced as I still was there in my engineering school days.

"Gerald," he said, pointing the tip of a sharpening file toward me. "Every day, every day, every day."

"Every day?" I said.

"Every day, son," Wendell Washington said. "You heard what I say. Every day."

So when my wife's parents got us moved into Terry Village at the University of Arkansas, a series of army barracks painted yellow and converted into apartments for married students, kissed their daughter goodbye, and pulled off in their pickup, I felt a deep and chilling fear descend upon me as I stood beside the road out. The gravel roadbed was bare and empty, a child's cry came from one of the apartments for graduate students and their broods, no birds sang, and I knew I was truly on my own with no excuses for failure. I had to make it here, and there was no one within 500 miles who gave a damn whether I did or not.

"This is a real crappy place," my wife said, looking through the doorway of building twenty-seven, apartment three of Terry Village. She was dead right, so I began explaining to her in detail why she was wrong, listening to myself speak and waiting to be persuaded that what I was saying was true. *Come on, belief, kick in,* I begged. *Give me something to keep me going. I know how to fool myself. Let's do it.*

The eleven months I spent earning a master's degree at the University of Arkansas seemed much longer than the calendar would indicate. I read every day in every spare moment from early morning to midnight. I taught my first class of students, a collection of people I hope I never see ever again because of my ineptitude in that first classroom. The course was designed for students in need of remedial reading skills, and my job was to help them read faster, better, and with more comprehension.

To aid me in that impossible assignment, special machines that moved text along at varying speeds were provided for each of the students in the classroom, and my job was to encourage individual adaptation as I increased the rate of flow of words across their monitors. I would stand in front of the room at the controls, turning the gauges that regulated each station as the heads of the group before me wobbled back and forth trying to keep pace. It was a horrible and pitiful sight to behold.

As I moved the gauge for individual students, they would increase the rate of their hopeless sprints to keep up, the hairdos of the women thrashing to and fro as though recording graphically an increasing fit of anger. Many of the men would simply stare straight ahead, eyes fixed on infinity, hoping for death. At the beginning of each hour I delivered little sermons exhorting these unfortunates to read faster, better, and with more comprehension, and when I exhausted what I had to say, I would direct them to stick their heads in the machines before them on their desks.

The collective groan that arose at my command to engage with the machines could have been little different from what prisoners in a medieval setting would have uttered at being told to get back on the treadmill because the lord of the manor required a greater flow of water to be pumped into the castle's kitchen. Cook needed more supply.

I was so afraid of the students and the questions they put to me that I acted like a Nazi taskmaster, refusing to smile or cajole or respond helpfully to any issues raised by any one of my charges. It was a war between them and me to see who would survive the ordeal of our sessions together, and I was determined to win.

In those years of higher education, teacher evaluations by students had not been dreamed of, and I was lucky on that score. Had the students in my first class been allowed to register an assessment of the quality of instruction or the competence of the teacher, I would have been ridden out of Fayetteville on a rail. I wouldn't have protested that action. I knew how bad I was, but funding for my graduate work depended on my coming to class each day and making those heads jerk back and forth at a faster and faster rate, and I did it, by God.

The courses in which I was enrolled demanded a great deal of reading and some writing, and I had no problem with any of that. It was easy, and I knew it, having served a two-year sentence in the college of engineering at Lamar, so when my fellow graduate students complained about the workload and its difficulty, I agreed but I was lying. Having to read a lot of books and write and talk about them was nothing compared to calculating the flux about a given point of an electrical circuit when the current surged. I could do graduate work in the study of literature standing on my head.

By the beginning of the second semester, I knew I wanted to go elsewhere to work toward a doctorate. I was better than most of the students in the English graduate program at Arkansas, and I was driven as always to try for a better certification of my worth. I had not chosen Arkansas by researching which programs most interested me or offered the best fit for what I wanted. All I wanted to do was get out of the Lone Star State of Texas, and I thought that any institution of higher education that called itself a university was roughly on a par with any other with the same label.

I went to Arkansas because I had previously visited a friend of mine a year older who had graduated from Lamar and was enrolled in sociology. The University of Arkansas looked like what I had seen in movies. It had hills and trees and old buildings, all of which were missing in the junior-high school architecture and overall affect of Lamar, and the bars near campus were full of good-looking Arkansas girls.

When I applied there, was accepted, and offered a teaching assistantship, I felt singled out for distinction, not realizing Arkansas was simply looking for cheap labor to make a set of students move their heads back and forth at a faster and faster rate until they were ready to go on to major in business and education.

Once there, though, and seeing how easily I succeeded, I thought I'd try to swim in a bigger and more prestigious pond, prove myself to be even more worthy of compliment and applause, and amaze old acquaintances and enemies by the further rise of a Duff in the big world outside East Texas.

I went to my professor of romantic poetry, a good-natured blowhard who was easy to flatter and a man who, to my amazement, was attractive to female students, and sought his advice. I instinctively knew he'd be flattered, though I didn't plan my approach cold-bloodedly, and he was that.

"Dr. Ivy," I said, "I think I'd like to leave Arkansas and go to Vanderbilt to work on my doctorate."

"Why Vanderbilt, Mr. Duff?"

"That's where Robert Penn Warren and John Crowe Ransom and Allen Tate are, isn't it?"

"No, they've all been gone from there forever," Dr. Ivy said. "Go to the University of Illinois. That's where I went."

So I applied, was admitted, and offered a teaching assistantship, and again I felt singled out for special recognition, not realizing that Illinois had its own set of freshmen needing to be taught on the cheap.

I passed my oral exams for the MA in English at the University of Arkansas early in August, and at the end of the month I pulled out of Fayetteville in an old Chevrolet sedan towing a rental trailer headed north. My seven-months-pregnant wife sat beside me, bracing herself against the dashboard each time I touched the brakes, since they were shot, and we were on our way to the big school in the middle of the cornfields. I would write my first novel about that corn.

CHAPTER 26

A Foreign Student in Illinois

WHEN I PULLED INTO CHAMPAIGN-URBANA, THE ARRIVAL WAS SUDDEN. THE month was August, and the corn in the fields was as high as an elephant's eye, as the Broadway song proclaims, so that the city with the huge university at its heart rose up abruptly in the midst of a sea of green stalks, brown tassels, and ears full of kernels as we entered town. It was an island in an ocean of field corn, the kind not fit for human consumption but just the ticket for hogs and the manufacturers of fructose. I was shocked and afraid and near comatose, and we were in immediate need of a place to live.

What we found that we could afford, until I got my first paycheck from the university for keeping forty of its freshmen occupied with the writing of essays, were two rooms of a duplex in somebody's backyard. Dried cereal was scattered on the floors of both rooms, the signs of a quick departure by the previous occupant, and I spent my first half-day in the major seat of learning in the Prairie State scraping up cornflakes fused to linoleum.

We weren't there long, able to move right before the birth of our first child into student/staff housing on campus. When the birth pangs hit my wife, I learned quickly that the hospitals of that Yankee state wouldn't allow entrance of patients, even a woman about to deliver, until they had an insurance card or cash money in hand. I borrowed $200 from a bemused banker who asked me if I was a foreign student. I insisted I wasn't, I just sounded that way, and that I was an American citizen to the core and good for the money in installments of twenty dollars a month. He signed me up, told me he had visited Houston once and found it too hot to bear, and we were in the baby-producing business in a hospital in Champaign.

Stuart arrived in the fall of 1962 during the week in which the United States and the USSR almost destroyed the world, and a fellow graduate student from Massachusetts urged me to name my first child *Cuban Crisis Duff*. Instead I settled for Stuart since I was reading John Stuart Mill's *On Liberty* that day, and I liked the sound.

In addition to the graduate student from Massachusetts, I found myself thrown in with many other strange outlanders. They were from all over the United States, some even from England and France and Spain, and they had gone to colleges and universities little like what I was accustomed to. The person most like me was a black woman from Virginia, who talked with no trace of the accent I heard from blacks in Texas or Maryland, and I realized from that fact that you could choose to sound different from the way you had learned to speak growing up. It could be a matter of choice and will. But there would be consequences.

When the department of English held a reception for all the new graduate students to let them meet each other, the faculty, and assorted administrators, the black woman from Virginia asked if she could accompany me and my wife to it, since she was as filled with trepidation about these strange people as we were. When Stuart was born, she visited our apartment to meet the new baby, bringing with her a gift of all the pennies from her piggy bank, and asking in return if she could have the dried scab which had by that point fallen off Stuart's healed navel. I was glad to let her have that, figuring she had her uses for such a mojo unknown to me.

Most radical, academically, for me was a requirement at the University of Illinois that all candidates for a doctorate in English had to endure successfully three semesters in the study of Anglo-Saxon, *Beowulf* in the original, and the history of the English language. The philologists had seized power early in the nineteenth century, maintained it, and had no plans of relinquishing it. If a student made As in all three courses, he was not required to pass the "philology" exam set for all aspirants to the PhD. The pressure was on from the beginning of the first day of the three semester sequence, one way or the other. If you made an A in Anglo-Saxon, you simply had to make As in the other two. If you didn't make an A in the Anglo-Saxon course, the doom of execution by philology exam was a few years away, stern and inevitable and quite possibly fatal.

Our instructor in Anglo-Saxon was a famous old scholar in the field, C. L. Wrenn, who wrote the book. He was visiting from Oxford for a year at Illinois, he was aged and white-haired and dressed in a tweed suit and a dirty yellow shirt, and he went around the room asking all of us aspiring Anglo-Saxon scholars where we had studied before coming to Illinois to pursue the doctorate.

"Cornell," the first man answered, and C.L.Wrenn approvingly named scholars of note at that institution. Other august names followed—Michigan, Stanford, Virginia, Iowa, UCLA—and the pattern set by Dr. Wrenn continued.

He knew someone eminent, renowned, able, and instrumental at every institution previously attended by this collection of students at Illinois. I sat and waited until he reached me, thinking of Polk County, Texas, the Round Stand at Marshall Hall, Maryland, and my professors at Arkansas.

"Next gentleman," the father of Beowulf said, looking over his weird English glasses at me. "Your name and your previous institution, please sir."

"Gerald Duff," I got out, and then, "The University of Arkansas."

"Arkansas," C. L. Wrenn said. "Arkansas. I've heard of that state. Is there indeed a university in Arkansas?"

UCLA, Stanford, Michigan, and Iowa chuckled, but Cornell sat quietly. I said nothing other than coloring prettily, I suppose, and the next person was asked the source of his most recent degree.

"Harvard," he announced. "In Cambridge, Massachusetts."

"I know where that's located, yes," C.L Wrenn said, and proceeded to list the name of eminences there. "But one question I have for you, Sir," he continued. "If you were at Harvard for your last degree, what are you doing now at Illinois?"

Cornell laughed at that loudly, and Arkansas joined politely.

CHAPTER 27

Not the Thing, But the Thing about the Thing

THREE THINGS NEW TO MY EXPERIENCE DOMINATED MY FOUR YEARS OF GRADUATE study at the University of Illinois. One was the physical cold of the winters, another was the growing mental illness of my wife, and the last was the way Illinois graduate study taught me to look at literature. All finally fell together into a heap.

I was constantly shocked when I had to venture outside a warm place to move to another building and face the wind cutting across the prairie full of ice and snow. I witnessed a growing separation between my wife and me as she moved further into herself and away from the world of daily life and other people. I was made to realize by my well-published and nationally recognized professors of English that what was important were not works of literature but what had been, and what could be, written about those works of literature.

It became all of a piece for me. These brute facts defined my existence and melted into one: the harshness of the barren winter prairie; the violently oscillating mood swings of the woman with whom I brought children into the world, and the fact that the time I had to devote to intellectual pursuit had better be spent on determining and absorbing what somebody had written about a poem, a novel, a play rather than reading more original works of the imagination.

In the springs and summers, I dreaded the Illinois winters to come and the bleakness those dead times represented to me. In the increasingly rare moments between my wife and me when we weren't regarding each other as though we were different species forced somehow to live together, I expected at any point to descend into shouting darkness. When I stopped on the way to my carrel in the stacks of one of the major university libraries in the world to sneak-read an unassigned novel or some other work irrelevant to the success of my pursuit of the doctorate, I felt I was performing a secret act of mental masturbation.

In my four years in the middle of the state of Illinois, I moved from apartments to houses to apartments with my growing family. I badly taught hundreds of uninterested freshmen the rudiments of writing dull essays on dull topics. I consumed all I was assigned to read from the works of scholars writing about other scholars writing about writing, while surreptitiously dipping into novels not in my field, and I wrote a doctoral dissertation about a subject in which I had no interest simply because it was a topic not yet plowed to powder by others.

I realized the depth of my despair one night at a New Year's Eve party with a bunch of other graduate students and their wives, the children of that drunken bunch asleep in piles in back rooms. At the hour of midnight, the couples around me and my wife paired off for the kissing traditional to the occasion. I turned toward my wife, and we simply looked at each other, no more a pair than an aardvark and a swordfish.

"Happy New Year," I said.

"Right," said my legal spouse, the mother of my children.

I lived in fear that the edge on which I walked would crumble beneath me, and I escaped that dread as much as possible by complete devotion to doing exactly what graduate study demanded, by reading what was written about other writing, and by adding my bit to the mass already accumulated. I was good at that limited task, and in the opinion of those that mattered I was a great success.

I left Illinois in four years with the PhD, two children, a wife beginning a slide into full-blown schizophrenia, and appointment as an assistant professor at Vanderbilt University. There they loved literature for its own sake, I believed. Hadn't all those famous literary names come from Vanderbilt, the Harvard of the South? Tate, Warren, Ransom, the Fugitives, the Agrarians. And wasn't that institution as far removed in character from East Texas as you could get? And only ten years earlier, hadn't I ridden in the open bed of a borrowed truck moving my mother and my father and my sisters from the pine barrens of Polk County to the Gulf Coast? Hadn't I risen? Hadn't I come far? Wasn't I about to get to where I belonged?

It would be good in Nashville at Vanderbilt. I would be Dr. Duff, and I would be a scholar of the English Romantic Period, and my wife and I, along with our children—Stuart and Audrey—would be just like everybody else in that fortress of academia.

CHAPTER 28

Fugitive at Vanderbilt

We got there all right, moved into the home of a professor of philosophy on sabbatical for a year, and I left each morning dressed in a coat and tie, carrying a briefcase full of student papers and textbooks, to perform the duties of a new assistant professor at Vanderbilt University.

I did not belong at Vanderbilt, and it took me years after I had been fired from that institution to realize and accept that. The department of English was chaired by an outsider new to the South and to his job, a bowtie-wearer from Princeton who wrote about Shakespeare in the most affected, stilted, and preciously twisted prose style ever produced by a native speaker of the language. He had utter contempt for the older faculty in the department, for good reason, and he was eager to demonstrate that opinion at every opportunity, often and effectively enough to ensure that every assistant professor he hired during his three years at Vanderbilt was discharged as soon as possible.

I was one of those, but I would not have lasted at Vanderbilt even if I hadn't been seen as one of the Ivy League chairman's boys and thus subject to death by tenure. Although I didn't realize it at the time, in my first week at Vanderbilt I was marked for execution by one of the old boys of the university. He was a graduate of the place, thus as dangerous in his character and in the certitude of his beliefs about the nature of Vanderbilt as a Bible-toting Baptist is about the inerrancy of the Word. Never have I seen an exception to this rule. He who returns to teach in the institution where he earned his first degree will prove to be a scoundrel.

On that afternoon, I was walking out the front door of Old Central, the original mansion where the university was given its seat by Cornelius Vanderbilt, a famed pirate of his day, when I was approached by the professor of creative writing in the English department. He grinned widely—as was his wont with one and all—showing his outsized orange teeth, and said in a gravelly upper-class middle Tennessee yodel, "Gerald, an old Texas boy like you, who're your people?"

Being an old Texas boy like me, I didn't know what Walter meant by the term "your people," so I responded much as I had when the Nederland High School guidance counselor asked me what my father did for a living. "Oh," I told Walter, "my father's a working man in the oil industry around Beaumont. Always has been." I thought by that admission I would escape having to tell the truth about how far Big Willie Duff had sunk, working as he did in his last years of employment in the Streets and Alleys and Waste Disposal Department for the City of Nederland.

But I did not impress Walter, who up to that point was prepared to accept me as a fellow Southerner if "my people" were of the right sort. When he learned that they weren't and when it became clear to him that I had drifted into friendship with the closet homosexuals in the department and the one Jew—a New Yorker who talked knowledgeably about art, music, leftist causes, and seventeenth-century poetry—I was no longer viewed by Walter as salvageable. I didn't know that this judging of my breeding was taking place at the time, not being up on the intricacies of the classification dance performed by upper-class Southerners who have learned to read, but it was on in full force.

The class system in the Vanderbilt English department was made even more complex than in other universities in the South in that day by the history of the great literary success that had defined the university early in the century. The ones who were the poets, novelists, and essayists of such distinction had long ago departed Vanderbilt, most of them fired or driven out by other means, and this fact meant that those oldsters who were left to tend the dying embers were the hangers-on, the would-be literary lions, and the sycophants and lickspittles that exist in any organization defending a fixed notion of its unchangeable character and august definition.

Let not a gray hair fall, nor a cracked urn crumble lest all the world be lost. That was the ethos of the department of English at Vanderbilt which I joined at age twenty-seven. I was therefore doomed the first day I walked on the campus. I didn't know that then, so I had some good times, met some people with whom I've formed lifetime friendships, and learned to look closely at individual works of literature to understand what was being said, how it was intended, and how its effects were accomplished. I became a New Critic, and that is the best thing that can happen to a teacher of the written word. I learned that there existed a literary text separate from me and my psychosocial, economic, and ethnic definition, and that close examination and thought could yield insight into that work of art.

I have clung to that simple-minded opinion in all things literary since that time, despite all onslaughts of new and improved ways to consider and celebrate the prominence of theory and the irrelevance of the text, and I have done so like a foot-washing Baptist in Camp Ruby, Texas. Jesus said it, I believe it, and that settles it, as the bumper stickers on the pickup trucks of my people declare.

I learned at Vanderbilt how to teach literature, and I wrote my first poems and short stories, began writing my first novel, watched my children begin to grow, and witnessed my first wife, along with our marriage, disintegrate in mind and selfhood.

Indian Giver I began when I was at Vanderbilt, stealing time from what should have been the serious work of a literary scholar, that of delving into sources and checking facts, footnotes, prior assessments, and modest assertions, all in the service of arriving at a small and considered contribution to the tiny advancement of an obscure bit of knowledge.

Instead, I remembered an Indian boy, a member of the Alabama-Coushatta Nation living on the reservation about five miles from the location of where I lived with my family in the piney woods of Polk County. He was Gustin Batiste, and I first saw him standing beside the highway as I rode in the school bus used to transport us scholars back and forth to Livingston each day. He was dressed in a long-sleeved red shirt and khaki pants, not the uniform used by white kids of the era, and I remember him always wearing that outfit each day of the time I knew him.

The bus driver, Carey Williams, a cold-eyed thin country man with no chin, stopped the bus and asked the Indian boy if he wanted a ride. He nodded and got on board, under the scrutiny of all of us. No other members of the Alabama-Coushatta Nation at that time went to school in Livingston—a full fifteen miles from the reservation—attending instead Big Sandy, a district that enrolled only a few hundred students in all twelve grades, and an academic outfit considered undistinguished by all who knew it. Except for one thing. They could forevermore play basketball, and the source of their ability to beat teams from all over that part of Texas, including huge Houston schools with hundreds of players from which to pick the best, were the young men of the Alabama-Coushatta Nation.

I never knew why Gustin Batiste chose to leave Big Sandy for the bigger and supposedly better school of Livingston, but he did. He and I grew to know each other, since I was the only one who wanted to sit by him on the bus each day, and I asked him questions about who he was and where he lived and what it was like to be an Indian and what meant what in his language. Some of these he deigned to answer, and some queries I made led him either to simply look at me without a word of response or to turn his attention to the scenery visible through the bus window. Pine trees, thickets, swamps, occasional houses, broken down cars and trucks, basketball goals nailed to posts, and other blank spots on the way to school.

After I moved from the barrens of Polk County I never saw Gustin Batiste again, but after I finished graduate school at Illinois, I imagined his being recruited to play basketball in the Big Ten at that university, coming from the reservation to do so, excelling at the game, failing at fitting the categories of identity demanded of him, and returning home to build a basketball goal deep in an uncleared thicket of the Alabama-Coushatta Nation where it would be impossible to play the game properly. I called his story *Indian Giver,* for obvious reasons, even though the editors told me the title was demeaning to Native Americans.

I wrote the book in Tennessee and in Ohio, I dedicated it to Gustin Batiste, and I was never able to find him to give him a copy. But I witnessed him play basketball, and I rode the bus with him every day. I saw a short obituary for him in the Polk County Enterprise. His name was misspelled, and basketball was not mentioned.

In my six years at the Harvard of the South, the great cultural revolutions of the late '60s occurred as well, and I was touched enough by that seismic shift to teach the first course in black literature ever offered at Vanderbilt, to grow a mustache and long hair, and to switch from wearing coats and ties in the classroom to sporting T-shirts and jeans. That shift in proper attire was certainly less expensive, a wondrous and good thing.

The sexual aspect of the revolution passed me by, though, since working full-time and tending to two children while my heavily-medicated wife spent weeks and months in a variety of mental hospitals, asylums, and group homes didn't leave time for me to consider dalliance outside the bounds of legal marriage.

I was too busy going into debt to pay doctors and hospitals and pharmacists, feeding and transporting children to schools and playgrounds, teaching a full load of classes, trying to write articles and books about what other people had already written articles and books about to better effect, and sneak-reading and sneak-writing fiction and poetry to be able to take advantage of the increased erotic opportunities of America in that golden age of birth control pills when HIV was not yet in view.

It was a cold and celibate time. One of my wife's doctors directed me in one of my many sessions of learning how to deal with the mental illness of a mate not to approach my wife sexually. I looked at him in amazement, marveling at his innocence, and told him not to worry. I hadn't been able to do that for years, and never expected to do so again. Sublimation of the sexual instinct had been and would continue to be my mode until I was freed by divorce the same year I was bankrupted financially, fired from my job at Vanderbilt, and forced to leave my children in the custody of a woman who hadn't been able to care for herself for years.

In the Tennessee courtroom, where the divorce action was accomplished on a clear fall day in 1971, the judge looked at me in sorrow tinged with a Solomonic weight of self-assurance and announced that the two children at issue were to be left to the mother. "The proper situation of minor children must be with the mother, who is by definition best suited to perform the duties of care and rearing of them. A Christian home setting provided by the mother is the best assurance for their future development and success."

In Tennessee at the time, the only grounds for divorce were those of a grievous and illegal fault of one or other of the married pair. Since my wife was suing for divorce, with which I was in total agreement, I had to find friends who would testify to my having been somehow actionably offensive in the relationship. Adultery was the ticket, since it was easily assumed and believed. I had to lie about messing around. I asked two members of the Vanderbilt English department to so perjure themselves on my behalf, and they did.

"Don't ever ask me to lie for you again, Gerald," one of my friends said, "especially in front of a judge."

"But, Jim," I replied, "sometimes a lie is the best friend you can have. I have spent a lifetime depending on what not telling the truth will do to get me by."

"I'm not from East Texas," Jim said. "Thank God."

CHAPTER 29

A Fortunate Fall

My first wife got what she wanted, the ability to seek a new and better life, as she has been able to continue doing in her next six marriages scattered over forty years, and I got what I wanted in reference to that first union. The cost was great. My children and I were apart, save for frequent visits and summer stays with me, for the next three years. But at the end of that period, I was able to rescue them from living with that mother judged so suitable for the care and rearing of offspring by the good Christian judge of the domestic court of metropolitan Nashville.

Everything was happening to me and mine at once in late 1971 and most of 1972. Life came in salvos, thoroughly and rapidly. The divorce was filed and granted, I achieved true financial bankruptcy, I was not recommended for tenure by a majority of the senior professors of the Vanderbilt English department, and I moved into a small apartment near the house where my children lived with their mother.

In that small apartment, I had a telephone on which I began to receive calls from a number of women who knew my new status, and a call from Robert Daniel, the chairman of the English department at Kenyon College, who was looking for a Romanticist. I was just the man for all those expressions of interest, and I devoted myself to proving my qualifications for that romantic label, broadly defined.

In my trip to Ohio for the job interview at Kenyon College, I was picked up at the airport by a college driver for the fifty-mile journey from Columbus to Gambier, and I stared out the car window all the way to Kenyon at the drifts of snow and the desolation of the farms and bleak villages. The scene both comforted and appalled. After finishing my study at Illinois, I had promised myself I would never live again in the Midwest, and here I was, even deeper into the landscape this time, and glad of it.

The South had proved to be much more complex culturally at the level of defining people at, in, and around a place like Vanderbilt, and I had failed to negotiate successfully the hidden shoals, rocks, sunken wrecks, and sudden drop-offs of those deceptively warm seas. Ohio would be easier, I knew, and my brand of redefining and recasting reality would go down well in a place as small and innocent as Kenyon College. After all, that was where John Crowe Ransom had sought refuge after being driven out of Vanderbilt. He had prospered and accomplished, and he was still alive there in the village of Gambier. I could do the same on a lower level, I told myself. I knew I could.

After dinner at the chairman's house, meetings the next day with department members, students, and administrators, I was offered the job. A month earlier, I had already been offered an appointment at a higher rank and a higher salary at the University of Southern Mississippi in Hattiesburg, but there was no doubt about where I would go. I had had my fill of Southern academe, and the difference in prestige between Kenyon and Southern Mississippi was obvious. I have always wanted more and better certification of my worth, ever since my purgatory in Polk County, Texas, defined with immaculate clarity for me by Aunt Rosalie's grudging gift of those four pieces of light bread my mother made me beg. My hunger cannot be satisfied.

So I was going to Kenyon, and the response of the senior members of the Vanderbilt English department to the news was sweet. Kenyon was an "other Eden" in their eyes, the place where Ransom landed after the expulsion from the Garden, where he founded the *Kenyon Review,* taught Robert Lowell and Peter Taylor and a distinguished army of other poets, novelists, and critics. Duff was going there. Duff, the one with no people. The one married to and now divorced from that crazy woman who acted strange at social functions. Duff, with his long hair, his ill-clad children, and his perverse interest in Nigra lit. He, that one.

As Brother James, back in the Camp Ruby, Texas, Baptist Church might have said, "Vengeance is mine, thus saith the Lord."

Soon after I moved to Gambier all my belongings in two boxes and on a clutch of wire hangers, I remarried, this time to a woman I had met in Nashville shortly before leaving the city. She was several years younger than I, she was eager to be married after a series of unsatisfactory relationships, and she was gainfully employed as a computer programmer. She was all that my first wife was not.

She liked my children, who liked her (immediately after meeting her, my six-year-old daughter asked if this woman could be her "new mama," breaking my heart upon the instant of my hearing the question), and she left her single life in Nashville without much of a look back. My new wife was industrious, capable, and determined to create what she imagined to be a proper and satisfyingly conventional domestic life. For two years, she and I drove back and forth to Nashville to visit my children, had them live with us on holidays and during the summers, and finally were able to have them moved to Gambier for good. Stuart came first, and in a few months, Audrey followed.

My son's move came when he announced to his mother that he was going, and my daughter's move to permanent residence in Gambier came as the result of a fortunate fall, a tumble off a skate board which broke her left arm. In a cast, she was unable to leave us to return to Nashville at the end of the summer upon doctor's orders. Or so I informed her mother back in Nashville, a lie that served me and my children well.

We put her in school in Ohio, where she immediately excelled academically and socially, being named the best student in her grade in an honors ceremony at the end of the year, and she never again lived with her biological mother. Her experiences in social diplomacy served her well over the years, and she became a woman who can handle any situation involving human beings or creatures aspiring to that label.

Her brother Stuart proved to be gifted mathematically and musically, unlike his father, and entered into the ranks of the successful computer geeks.

Their mother back in Nashville was by that point deep into a third marriage, with four more to follow over the years, and she was not concerned enough about the children to protest their unofficial but lasting shift to living with me. It worked out well for all concerned, and my agonies of separation from my children were at an end.

Teaching at Kenyon proved to be worlds better than what I had experienced at Vanderbilt. The English department was the largest and best at the college, attracting the best students who, for the most part, read what they were assigned, wrote well, and considered themselves to be where they belonged. So did I, and I spent the rest of my professional career, the one in which I made enough money to support my family, send them to college, and amass enough capital to retire at the end of 2007, in small colleges.

I no longer had to hide my poetry and fiction, either, at Kenyon, where anything productive by a faculty member was recognized and valued. I could have happily spent the rest of my teaching career there, basking in the easily won regard of students of literature, publishing short stories, novels, and poems, and working with the *Kenyon Review,* except for one solid fact. My second wife realized she didn't like living in the bucolic isolation of a small liberal arts college more than fifty miles from any community with a population of more than a few thousand people, and she made her dissatisfaction vividly apparent.

She came from a socioeconomic background much different from mine. Her father was a banker in Atlanta, a mover and shaker in the community, fulfilling such roles as board chairman of the new MARTA rail system in the city, serving as leader of boards and civic organizations, and as shining example to his daughter of what a successful man should be. He was admirable in all ways, decent, forward-looking, and kind to his biological grandchildren and to his step-ones as well.

His son took a different path and succeeded stunningly, but his daughter wanted to be like her father and prided herself on every manifestation of similarity between her characteristics, her career goals, and those of her father.

Living and working in Gambier, Ohio, being mother to two stepchildren and wife to me, and not having her abilities challenged and rewarded were too much for her to be satisfied in our marriage. She announced to me that if I didn't find a job in a Southern city (preferably Atlanta), which would allow her what she needed, that our relationship would be over. So I went to work on trying to do just that, sending out applications every year to every suitable possibility, and I finally succeeded in finding a way out of Gambier.

What distance in time and space provides a novelist is a certain ambivalence of effect. It allows both for a cooling-off period, an opportunity to acquire a more balanced perspective on old wounds and new healing, but it also affords the chance to sharpen one's knives and study the most hurtful areas for application of the blades. Someone once said that revenge is a dish best served cold. The passage of time and the removal to a location away from the scene of defeat and disillusionment are thus good friends to the novelist of satiric intent.

Those sentiments are most appropriate to *Graveyard Working,* my second novel, and the one most directly aimed at people of kin, at events, and at situations endured during my childhood years in East Texas. I take an axe to family in that one, a book I wrote most of in Gambier, Ohio, finishing it in Memphis while I waited for *Indian Giver* to be published.

After it was complete, I called my sister to express concern that one or two of my elderly aunts might be insulted by some of the occurrences and characterizations in the book, uncomfortably close to teetering on verifiable fact as they might be.

"What do you mean?" Nancy said. "What are you afraid of?"

"Well," I said, "you know. I make some of them look pretty bad. Saying and doing some low-minded stuff, you understand."

"Oh, I see," my sister said. "You think one of our aunts might see herself in it, huh?"

"Well, yeah."

"Gerald, you know they don't read."

She was right, of course, and now they're all dead anyway, and some reviewers of the novel remarked at the time that what I was striving for in the novel was an especially over-the-top Southern Gothicism. Real people couldn't act like the ones in *Graveyard Working,* the reviewers implied, and I was simply working some more of the ground already so well plowed by Faulkner and Flannery O'Connor, and the effects were "grotesquely amusing," as the *Atlantic Monthly* lady put it.

Nuh-uh, as my people in deep East Texas would say. *I ain't just a wolfing.*

In the meantime, my wife's father had died of a sudden massive heart attack at age sixty, her mother, who deserved, and in fact has had, a book written about her (a wonderfully sensitive and upsetting psychological study from her son), had begun to call her daughter almost nightly in the small hours after midnight to complain about her abandoned state and her ungrateful children.

The last several years of my time at Kenyon were hard on us both, husband and wife, and the marriage collapsed soon after I resigned from Kenyon and left for Memphis.

At Kenyon, though, I had finished writing my first novel, published a first collection of poems and two scholarly books, taught for a year as a visiting lecturer at the University of Exeter in England, raised my children to teenagedom, and become financially solvent. It was a good eight years. I had gotten well. Like Rabbit Angstrom, I was *redux*.

CHAPTER 30

As Kool-Aid Is from Gin

We bought a house in Memphis in Central Gardens, the venue of many of Peter Taylor's best stories, and we moved to the Bluff City for me to begin my job as chief academic officer (dean to ordinary folks) at Southwestern at Memphis. All the way to Memphis, as we drove in two cars—my wife and I in the lead one and the children in the other, proudly driven by seventeen-year-old Stuart—my wife wept continuously as we worked our way south, demonstrating an amazing capacity for tears. Memphis may have been a Southern city, but it wasn't Atlanta. Most important, it was several hundred miles from the City Too Busy to Hate and from her family's cabin on a beautiful lake in the northern part of the state—the site of idyllic memories.

I had done what I could to get us located in a Southern city where my wife could find a real and a challenging job in keeping with her abilities and ambition, but Memphis was not the place. The marriage lasted only about eighteen months after we arrived in Memphis and moved into the beautifully renovated old house on Peabody Avenue in Central Gardens. She packed her belongings, had me ship her dog, Hannah More, to her by plane, and left for Concord, Massachusetts, a long way from Atlanta. But it was where the Digital Equipment Corporation, the high-tech organization at which she found suitable employment as a computer programmer, was situated.

Our separation and divorce were as amicable as those ruptures can be. I wasn't interested in her financial holdings, I had none of any consequence, and there was no contesting anything. In a few months, I moved with my daughter into a small house on the edge of Central Gardens, and my son began his studies at the college where I was dean. There were some bitterness and lasting animus toward me from my second wife, admittedly and deservedly, but she has maintained a loving relationship with the children she helped raise ever since she left Memphis, the Baghdad on the Mississippi, and moved to the outskirts of the most northern of cities in the United States, Boston.

Life as a dean at a small college in the South was as different from teaching English at Kenyon as Kool-Aid is from gin. I discovered that the first time I sat down at a lunch table of faculty members in the school cafeteria. They immediately fell silent, looked at their plates, ate their casseroles with speed and departed one by one for other duties. I would not be able to be one of them ever again, I realized, so I thought about the size of my salary and the fact that there was so much dead time in the forty hours of sitting behind my desk that I had no excuse not to write every day.

I did that. In the six years I was at Southwestern at Memphis, called SAM by its president until he was able to change the name to Rhodes, I published my second collection of poetry, my first novel, and wrote two others. *Indian Giver* was already finished after years of fiddling with it. The first one I wrote behind the desk in the dean's office was *Graveyard Working,* in which I took an axe to my extended family in deep East Texas, and the second was my first try at Memphis, a novel I called *That's All Right, Mama: the Unauthorized Life of Elvis's Twin.* All three of the novels served therapeutic ends for me, as all literary efforts do for every writer. But each ministered to its own separate and specific wound.

At the time, I was learning to deal with a real boss for the first time in many years—having been a college teacher since 1966 and thus, like all academics, in my own mind beholden to no man—I fell in love with a woman for the first time. She was from Alabama, she was beautiful, witty, intelligent, kind, and she loved me. She was Pat, and deserves a separate book, one apart from this one in total thrall and service to me alone. From the first, we were together, and are, and will be. She makes me understand why Shakespeare wrote his sonnets, and she cannot be captured in a few or in many paragraphs. She is beyond the word. No lie.

The first college president I worked for had been an English major in his undergraduate days, and he was proud of that, often remarking that he loved Wordsworth's "Lines Composed a Few Miles Above Tintern Abbey" so much that he read it each night before drifting off to sleep. Once I quoted the first line of that poem to him in greeting as we met on the campus, and he asked me where those words had come from.

He was also an ordained Presbyterian minister who had pastored churches before taking up his family business of carpet manufacturing in Georgia. After a few years, he became president of Southwestern at Memphis, a Presbyterian college, because as he put it in his inaugural address, "they offered me the job." The faculty at the college despised and feared him, their feelings springing from his non-academic background, I thought at the time. But later experience at other colleges showed me that faculties to one degree or another always hate and despise the president, no matter his or her background, experience, and character.

My first president was not an academic or an intellectual, but he could sell a product, and that he did in his job of boss of Southwestern at Memphis. His faculty contemporaries will never recognize his contributions, but future generations looking at what he wrought will arise and call him blessed. He taught me something about lying, a subject at which I considered myself expert, having learned through exigency and practice its beauties and utility. And that was this, to quote Emily Dickinson: "Tell all the truth but tell it slant." My first president did not tell bald lies, nor construct edifices of untruth, but he could put a spin on the pitch that made it do the downright dipsy-doodle as it neared home plate. You could not hit it, and if you put the bat on it at all, it became an easily played grounder.

I worked for two other college presidents as chief academic officer, second in command, playing the role of what my father would have called the "straw boss," and both CEOs were expert spinners of a story when need arose.

They could not compare to the president of SAM, however, in his ability to say a thing so persuasively to his proper audience that they would weep with joy as they reached for their checkbooks. He could forevermore bring it.

Like any petty king, he played favorites. All of us members of his Cabinet, as he called the group, were in a constant sweat about who was up and who was down. We didn't trust each other ever, and that lack of certainty was what his changing appraisals of us was designed to accomplish. One day early in my tenure at the college, the Vice President for College Relations asked me to come to his office for coffee, always a sign of looming distress in academe.

"Gerald," he said, "you're on top with him now. You can do no wrong, and you should take advantage of that."

"How? Ask for a raise?"

"No, he won't like that. If there's any pet project you want to push, now's the time to do it, while he still thinks you've hung the moon. But let me tell you, it will not last. Shifting his attention and removing his favor, that's the way he has fun."

I had no pet project, didn't want one, and didn't want to spend a minute of time thinking one up. I didn't tell the VP that, of course, since the overriding falsehood of life in an institution of higher learning is that each person there employed, from janitor to assistant professor to dean to president to chair of the board, has a burning desire to advance some act of selfless contribution to the overall good of alma mater. If only there were world enough and time.

There are many lies in higher education, but that's the big one. No one will admit otherwise. I once had an associate dean, one who reported to me and was a good hardworking man in all respects, say these words. "There is nothing I like better than thinking about curriculum."

"Just curriculum?" I asked. "Just that alone?"

"Oh, yes," he said, his eyes swimming in a near ecstasy of sincerity. I believe he thought he believed that, and that it was possible to think about curriculum as curriculum, but to me an apt parallel would have been Albert

Einstein saying, "I like nothing better than thinking about scientific thought."

At the time I expressed complete agreement with my associate dean about the beauties of curriculum *qua* curriculum, and in my talk with the VP for College Relations I assured him there were several selfless projects to the greater good of SAM I wanted, above all else in life, to advance. I was lying in both cases, but the lie is the coin of the realm in higher education management. It's almost as rampant as the mendacity purveyed in the classrooms of professors of the social science disciplines. It is the spine which holds all else upright.

Deaning at SAM allowed me to be in Memphis, however, and that proved to be richly rewarding in my attempts to write fiction. Memphis was and is an embodiment of the central paradox of the South. It is both tight and loose, and so are Southerners.

Memphis has more churches of every Christian denomination, in more locations, conducting more worship services, attended by more of the faithful, than any other comparably sized city in the nation. It is proud of that fact and lives out its implications each and every day.

Memphis also has more low dives and honky-tonks, more high and low bars, more prostitutes and drug houses, more robberies and gang shootings, more muggings and murders, just generally more of the fast life than any other city in the nation.

When I was being taken to dinner during my interview visit to Southwestern at Memphis, I was driven in the Mercedes of an associate professor of history to an expensive and tasteful restaurant in an old mansion downtown. As we rode along talking about curriculum, I suppose, we stopped at a light next to another expensive car, occupied by two attractive and well-dressed young African American women.

As I glanced over at them, the driver began to speak and to point toward our car, smiling and gesturing. Not able to hear what she was saying and thinking she had perhaps noticed some pending mechanical problem with the professor's Mercedes, I lowered the window and asked what she was saying. She spoke again, and the woman beside her in the front seat leaned across to add her voice.

"I couldn't understand you," I said. "What did you say?"

"I asked if y'all want a blowjob," she said, smiling prettily. Her friend opened her mouth wide and shoved a finger down her throat to illustrate graphically what I couldn't seem to understand.

"Not right now," said the associate professor of history, leaning across me to speak to the purveyors of head. "But thanks."

"Whores?" I said to him, as we pulled away.

"I do believe they are," he said as we headed for Justine's. "When you were at Vanderbilt, did you teach any graduate courses?"

That coexistence side by side of the sacred and the profane, the academic and the real, the job interview and the offer of a blowjob—this comfort with the bifurcated nature of the human—encapsulates what is the central truth about Memphis, Tennessee, the Bluff City. There are myriad intersections of different worlds occurring constantly in Memphis, and in fact and in fiction, these constitute the essential identity of the place.

If Nashville is about the greed for money and the drive to make it, Memphis is about giving in, abandoning all hope, and having a good time. If Memphis is a city whose basketball players cannot make free throws, Nashville is a city whose university's players can make only free throws.

At one point in its history, Memphis was poised to become a major American city, complete with manufacture, conglomerations of agriculture and business, shipping, building, and all that goes into making centers of commerce buzz and thrive. But something happened in the nineteenth century that dealt Memphis a body blow to all aspirations for serious material profit, and something happened in the twentieth century to finish off all hopes of grandeur.

The first of these calamities was the yellow fever epidemic which reduced the Memphis population to a fraction of what it had been and what it needed to prosper, and the second was the assassination of Dr. Martin Luther King, the finishing blow to Memphis's status as a contender in the big world of growth and commerce. For the hopers and planners, these disasters were apocalyptic, but for the writer, they created a climate and a culture conducive to dream, disillusionment, regret, and loss.

The advantages for the writer are clear and compelling. Vanity, all is vanity, endeavor is doomed, and success is fleeting, evanescent, and gone. Here is where satiric art thrives, not in the happy realms of cities that hold out hopes that may be realized and dreams that may become real. The writer of ironic fiction is at home in Memphis, not in Nashville or Atlanta or Minneapolis, much less in the fabled centers of energy and fulfillment on the American coasts.

In what other city can the African American mayor say openly, as Willie Herenton—the long time leader of the government of Memphis—did once, "There's not a thing the mayor of this city can do about crime," and get away with it? Willie said that, and Memphians of all colors concurred. "He got that right," was the universal response to the mayor's judgment that nothing could, or would, be done. Not here, not in Memphis.

Memphis is the city where rock and roll was born, and where it died. It is the city where the blues got their first hold in an urban setting, and it is the city where Beale Street is now a collection of Disney venues for Midwestern tourists. It is where the King Himself arose, combining the sounds of blacks and mountain whites into what defined the popular musical culture of America for the world to consume. And it is the location where the King of Rock died sitting on a toilet, his head buzzing with drugs and half-baked misconceptions about what he was and what he meant.

For me, a minor regional novelist unable to escape from Texas, Memphis and its overlapping and intersecting realities provided a rich brew for four of the works of fiction I've written and a sense that there's so much more to tackle if only I had the talent to do so. I hadn't lived there for a year before I realized I wanted to write a novel about Elvis Presley, knowing he was the key to getting my arms around some small part of what Memphis means.

At the end of a night of drinking, one of many I suffered and enjoyed in the Bluff City, I confessed to a friend, a successful writer visiting from New York, that I wanted to take on the task but that I had no idea how to begin. "How do you write a novel about Elvis," I asked. "He's too big and obvious and easy to ridicule. You can do a biography, you can analyze his poor white origins and the sources of his music, you can hold him up for admiration and marvel, and you can tear him down like a Mississippi sharecropper shack, but what do you end up with?"

"Write a novel about his brother," my friend said. "He had one, a twin, Jesse Garon, who died at birth. He'd be easier to hem up in a corner than the one that lived. He's a fiction in his own right."

That night I wrote on a Memphis Light, Gas, and Water bill the first two sentences of the novel. "I have never had the benefit of a mother's love. Elvis got it all."

It took a while before I got fully cranked up on my Jesse Garon novel, but when I did, I wrote it in nine months, working each morning at my desk in the dean's office at Southwestern at Memphis. I researched the book by plagiarizing the facts of Elvis's life from biographies, by visiting bars where Elvis impersonators performed, by listening to Elvis's music, all of it, including even such things as "Stay Away, Joe," "Peace in the Valley," and "My Way," and by remembering what it was like to grow up in East Texas.

That's All Right, Mama: the Unauthorized Life of Elvis's Twin was the only novel I wrote while living in the geographical location where the book is set. I think I understand why I wrote about Elvis Presley from the first-person perspective of his brother Jesse Garon while I was actually living as a citizen in Memphis. Being in the city where Elvis is still very much a living presence contributed strongly to what I was trying to do in that book, as I channeled, to use a term from pop psychology, the feelings of despair and unrealized chances of a fictional character on the edge of a recognition forever denied him.

In my novel, Jesse Garon functioned as the side of Elvis always just beneath the surface existence of an icon forever known to all the world. Elvis had made it to the status of myth and immortality by his public performance, his selfhood, and his status as a favorite of the gods, and that identity became immediately and always available for consumption. The other half of him, though, that of the dispossessed poor white boy from Mississippi who moved with his mother and father to Memphis in a simple search of a better life, is best captured for me by the self that died at birth. That self is Jesse Garon Presley, the first-born twin obliterated from earthly existence before a breath could be drawn.

As I wrote about that shadow self of the Elvis myth, I did so in the Mecca to which his father, a man who had served time in prison for forgery and hog theft, was drawn in hopes of another chance. I didn't need aesthetic or physical distance to imagine the early days in Memphis of that impoverished family, the loser father and the loving mother bound up in dreams of success for her son, and the strange misfit boy unsuited to compete with others in the arena of their comfort and fit. Memphis fed my imagination as I wrote the story of that life. And I had lived that life in deep East Texas in practiced deception.

I had only to visit the home which Elvis won, the palace named Graceland where he lived out the rest of his life with his parents, to sense the immensity and tawdriness of his dream, realized in the only way he could imagine it—a big house in Memphis with such testimony to success as white columns on the porch and a jungle room and television sets everywhere and a gold piano in the parlor. In Memphis as I worked on the novel, I could and did visit cheap night clubs filled with patrons avidly watching pitiful performances by impersonators of the King, I studied the memorial garden at Graceland with its maudlin inscriptions engraved on the bronze coverings of the graves of the Presleys, and I talked to people at all levels of Memphis society who claimed personal encounters of epiphanic meaning with the boy who had moved from Tupelo to live the full life in the Bluff City.

I wrote that novel in the immediacy and heat of the presence of what Memphis communicated to me, and I meant and understood what I intended in the way I imagined a dark and lost shadow twin would have fought for a life of his own.

When it was published, almost ten years later, the book did well critically and financially. The King still had it, and people wanted some more of it, from whatever slant a writer decided to give it to them. As soon as the book was out and reviews began to appear, I began to receive phone calls and letters from folks desperate to believe it was true that Elvis's twin had indeed survived, lived all those years as a shadow double to his brother, and was still out there doing gigs in low dives lost somewhere in America.

One call in particular said it all, waking me after midnight where I was living in Baltimore. "Is this the guy who wrote the book about Jesse Garon Presley?" the caller asked in a low and hopeful voice, in a minor key touched by the sound of many past disappointments.

"Yeah," I said. "That's me."

"Where is he? Jesse Garon, I'm talking about."

"That book is fiction. It's a novel."

"I know all that," the caller said. "I read that in the newspaper. My wife says it was in that *Entertainment Weekly* magazine, too. What I want to know is if you can tell me where Jesse Garon's playing right now."

"Well, in the last scene of the story I show him in Memphis," I said. "At the Vapors Supper Club."

"That's out in South Memphis, ain't it? Off Winchester?"

"Yeah, close to Bad Bob's."

"Thanks, Buddy," the caller said. "I hope I can get to Memphis before Jesse Garon leaves."

"Good luck," I said. "He doesn't stay anywhere long."

"Tell me about it," the voice said, and the caller hung up, travel plans in mind, I supposed.

My wife had awakened by then and heard most of the conversation, at least my end of it. "I wish you wouldn't do that," she said. "Feeding people's craziness is wrong."

"That's what a writer does," I told her. "It's my job."

"Bullshit," she said. "At least you didn't tell him where we live, did you?"

"He's not looking for me. He's looking for all that's left of the King. He's hunting for Jesse Garon. He's Memphis bound."

I have written three novels and several short stories and poems about Memphis, but I don't think I'm exhausted with the Bluff City yet. I do know, though, that however emptied of energy I may become, Memphis, that fever den on the big river, that home of lies and dreams and regrets, is not nearly played out yet.

I stayed at Southwestern at Memphis for six years, long enough for the president to rechristen the college as Rhodes, supposedly in honor of a former president, Peyton Nalle Rhodes, but we all knew that if the old boy had been tagged with a different label he wouldn't have had a chance to achieve such immortality. If he were a Strawberry or a Birthington or a Struggs or anything other than a Rhodes, Peyton would have had to be satisfied with his name being slapped on a minor building of the campus, if that.

My six-year tenure at Rhodes, née Southwestern at Memphis, was long past the point where the president had fallen out of love with my position as chief academic officer. He was fickle, and when he created the new position of provost designed to outrank me and put me firmly in my place, I knew it was time to go. So I left, but not before getting a call from my wife one morning when I was deep into some meaningless project in the dean's office.

"Stop whatever you're doing," she said, "and drive out to Jackson Avenue. Elvis is selling watermelons out of the back of an old Ford pickup. You've got to see him before we leave Memphis."

She was right. A perfect double for the dead King, dressed in overalls and blue work shirt, was hawking seedless watermelons, and I bought one to be able to talk to him, baldly saying, "Do you know you look just like Elvis?"

"Thank you, sir," he said with a modest chuckle. "People have told me that."

At that point a black kid not older than ten or eleven came wandering up, his gaze fastened on the man handing me the watermelon. "Hey, mister," he said. "Are you Elvis Presley?"

"No, son, I'm not," Elvis said in a regretful tone. "You want you a slice of watermelon?"

"Sure, Elvis," the kid said, and I left with my purchase, watching the black kid bite into his slice of watermelon in public, unabashed by fear of stereotype or a violation of correctness. The melon was sweet.

Memphis, Memphis. I was glad I had finally seen Jesse Garon on site before I left for Baltimore.

CHAPTER 31

Women Writing about Women Writing about Women

I TOOK THE JOB OF CHIEF ACADEMIC OFFICER AT A WOMEN'S COLLEGE IN Baltimore, fallen on evil days after a century of educating young ladies from up and down the east coast, and now about to become coeducational. It had to make that change to stay alive. So few young women would choose an all-female college by the 1980s that the marginal women's institutions were undergoing sex-change operations in droves.

The school that hired me had existed on the fringe of the famous Seven Sisters of women's colleges, the Smiths and Vassars and Wellesleys, but if it was a sister, she was an ugly duckling, small and slow-witted and a tad overweight. But as the president at Southwestern at Memphis had announced when asked why he had taken the job at that college, I took the offer in Baltimore because they made it to me.

I learned immediately that the faculty of a single-sex institution was a different breed from what I was used to at coed colleges. There were lots of female faculty, but they had a commitment to being female that was pronounced. They often declared themselves to be of that sex, as though they were being accused of masquerading as something else. Any fool could look at them and tell they were female, whether they wore makeup or not, or the ordinary dress of women or seaman's oilskins, but many of them were uneasy about being misidentified.

They never laughed. They never joked. They never flirted. By default, the male faculty members had the responsibility of carrying out these acts of cultural behavior, and most did that well. Both sexes of the faculty were suspicious of me, coming from Texas originally as I did, and having spent my entire career in coeducational institutions. I did little to assuage their fears, I confess.

Once an older member of the female faculty, a professor of political science who had spent some years in London and therefore pronounced the word *issue* in a manner never before heard in the English speaking world, told me about a coming conference.

"It is a gathering of those interested in women writing about women," she informed me, her mass of gray curls and her many necklaces a twitch and a jangle.

Trying to joke, I pretended to misunderstand. "Women writing about women writing about women?" I asked, and the old professor of political science jumped back as though she'd seen a rattlesnake or its human equivalent.

"I beg your pardon," she said, and I made things worse by using the word she pronounced so well, *issue*, but said it in a broad Texas drawl.

"I hope I haven't created an *issue*," I ventured.

Oh, well.

There were good things about working at the newly coeducational college, though, including the fact that no one came to work before 9:00 AM but me, and that there were so few students and such low expectations for faculty performance that I had little to do. I had plenty of time to write in my office, and I did so, completing a novel about the Bluff City called *Memphis Ribs*, one set on the Alabama-Coushatta reservation in Texas named *Snake Song*, and another set on the Gulf Coast of Texas, *Coasters*.

After finishing the third year and seeing the number of men at the college rise to only thirty-three in four years, I decided I had done all the damage I could do in that locale, and I resigned. I began teaching writing classes at Johns Hopkins University, where my wife had a faculty appointment in the School of Medicine, we took advantage of what Baltimore offered and the fact that everything is so close together on the East Coast, and we lived in Charm City for ten years.

Memphis Ribs, my genre-bending hard boiled comic mystery, as the flap copy describes the book, I wrote while living in Baltimore, a city I have attempted to put to fictional use in only one short story to date. F. Scott Fitzgerald once said of Baltimore, "I belong here where everything is civilized and gay and rotted and polite." Fitzgerald was Fitzgerald, though, and I have not yet tried to get my arms around more than twenty-five pages of fiction about the city. But I don't live there any more, and I may want to attempt it some day now that my perspective is cooled and less embroiled.

Memphis is different, and once I left its environs, I was emboldened to try to capture in fiction some of its toughness, violence, obsession with barbecue and beautiful women, its racism and restiveness, and its hard-edged hilarity. I did so by casting as a Memphis homicide cop a man in North Mississippi I had gotten to know. He was an independent cotton farmer, a Vietnam veteran who wasn't bothered in any discernible way by his year as a combat infantryman in country, and a man completely at ease with himself. He drank copious amounts of Crown Royal without seeming drunk, he loved his wife, and he had many friends, black and white, who admired him and gave him great room and latitude.

Reviewers liked that novel, too, and deemed it a great exaggeration of the city of Memphis, its culture of booze, barbecue, and blues, and called it a "hybrid of unsavory characters, seedy situations, and social satire." All I was trying to do was to show how Danny M would act if called upon to sort out crimes in the Bluff City. I was just sitting in the dean's office in Baltimore, enjoying the safety of distance and describing what I had seen in Memphis.

CHAPTER 32

Cousin Joseph Winston Tells the Truth

IF THE WRITING OF FICTION IS THE "CONSCIOUS CREATION OF A CONTINUOUS dream," as the novelist John Gardner once said, the dreams we have in actual sleep are a subset of lies, the way the unconscious mind works to make it possible for us to keep living with ourselves. Or so psychologists tell us with certitude, their assurance a lie in itself. Lies and the truth are close kin, though, particularly in deep East Texas, and a recent dream brought that truth home to me like an old wound reopened.

The dream was about my cousin, Winston, a relative I hadn't thought about in years. I awoke from it in the way you do when you're trying to escape a nightmare, a situation so disturbingly real your mind tells you to find a way to leave it as soon as possible. It's only a dream, you want to say. I'm not here. I'm in my bed asleep, and if I try hard enough I'll be conscious again in a place where I'm not dreaming.

I jerked awake, in a cool room with covers over me and my wife asleep beside me, and I waited for the calm of reality to reassure that all was well, no matter what my unconscious mind was telling me. The aftereffects of the dream lasted, though, much longer than ordinary, and even after I'd gone back to sleep, something worked inside to remind me of where I had been and how badly I had wanted to leave that place.

In the dream, Winston and I were in possession of a stolen car, a luxury auto of great solidity—massive, sleek and dark in color—and we were in a parking garage planning how we'd convert what we had into cash. My cousin had stolen the car, but I had arranged the theft and now I was terribly afraid I'd be found out. In the dream I was conscious of being myself in my current situation in life—a dean of a college with a reputation and social status to protect. A black man was there in the garage, colluding with us in this criminal act. He had Jheri curls, a ruined face, and he reeked of danger.

Winston was himself as I had last seen him, a day over twenty years before when he had come to my father's funeral in East Texas in a cemetery named Menard Chapel where members of the Duff family have been buried for generations, all the way back to the first family member in Texas, Winston's and my great-grandfather who had come to the state from Louisiana after his participation in the Civil War. He had become a Baptist preacher after the war, he founded the church at Menard Chapel, and he spawned all the Duff family to come.

Winston and I were the only sons of two brothers of the clan. I was four or five years older than Winston, and my first memory of him is as a child in my family's house in Nederland. He had been left for my mother to look after, and he had a cold so severe that snot was running down his face as he stood in our living room looking up at me, his older cousin, and trying to snuffle stuff back into his head.

"Look at Winston," I said to my mother. "Fix him. He's all messed up."

She tended to that, and I left the room, not wanting to be around somebody who looked like him, who was so repulsive and who wanted to follow me around in such a leaking condition.

Our family moved a lot, from one rent house to another in whatever locations in East Texas and in the petro-chemical area of the Texas Gulf Coast Big Willie Duff could find work, and Winston's family was worse in that respect than we were. My sightings of Joseph Winston Duff were scattered and infrequent, but always memorable, due largely to the fact that his father Lewis was a notorious drunk, liable to show up at any time of the day or night at the homes of his brothers and sisters in search of somewhere to lay his head and particularly to look for something to drink. Often he had Winston with him.

Uncle Lewis's only son was the fifth child born in the family, and his arrival was so momentous to Uncle Lewis—a boy at last, after the succession of daughters Emily, Betty, Doris, and Nola Mae—that he was given a special name. It wasn't until I was well along in my education that I realized why my cousin was named Joseph Winston, and I was amazed to recognize the source of his given names. He was born during one of the monumental diplomatic meetings of the Allies during World War II, and the names chosen by his father came from those of Joseph Stalin and Winston Churchill in light of their gathering with FDR in Yalta to divide up the Western world on the verge of the Allied victory in Europe.

Winston's naming was Faulknerian, I came to realize, akin to the sardonic name slapped on the character Wallstreet Panic Snopes by the novelist in one of his lesser books, and its choice reflected not thought, but a desire by an ignorant parent to lend an infant significance by labeling the child after a stray element in the Zeitgeist. It would have been embarrassingly laughable to anyone with a semblance of education and awareness, but that fact did not apply in the case of Lewis Calvin Duff, father of Joseph Winston. I imagine the names he chose for his only son sounded important, even august, to him, and he intended by the naming of his son to bestow a mark of respect and an homage to greatness by the act.

Joseph Winston had been singled out, and he had the label to prove it. He didn't realize that fact, but those in the social classes above him could be mildly entertained by what he was called, if they happened to notice it. That amusement of his betters would be an expression of contempt for him and his kind, but he was not likely ever to know that.

I was around Winston, off and on, until my family made its move from the Gulf Coast to the pine barrens of Polk County after my father lost his job with the Sun Oil Company and retreated to his home ground to sulk and plot vengeance. It wasn't until after we returned to the Golden Triangle, eight or nine years later, that I saw Winston for more than a couple of hours at a time.

My family, brought low by my father's inability to find regular work at a living wage, came back to Nederland so that my father could seek employment in a place that had jobs, and we stayed for a couple of weeks with Uncle Lewis and Aunt Myrtie and their children still at home. Those were Virginia Anne and Winston. Ginny Anne was a child still, but Winston had grown into a rangy, wide-shouldered youth, hungry for a different kind of food, real and metaphorical.

"Winston," I said to him soon after we'd moved in, "will your daddy let us use his lawn mower to go around and ask folks if we can cut their grass and make us some money?"

"I don't see why not," my cousin said. "He ain't going to be using it."

We took off every morning then with a gas can and the beat-up rotary mower, walking the streets of Nederland, Texas, looking for unmowed yards. Sure enough, we found a few people, mainly old ladies living alone as well as a few younger ones with husbands who either didn't own a mower or wouldn't use it, willing to hire us to mow their weedy St. Augustine grass-filled yards. Our most likely takers, we soon learned, were on the low end of the economic scale in Nederland, and they didn't want to pay much.

The nicer-looking yards belonged to people who gave us hard looks and short answers, no matter how badly their grass needed cutting, and we quickly learned to judge our low likelihood of success with this class of people and to keep moving when we saw signs of affluence: a nice car parked in the driveway, matching curtains in the windows, houses neatly painted, well-dressed children, women whose hair showed signs of having been messed with in beauty parlors, unbroken toys in the yard, and planted flowers in beds.

A typical rate for a grass cutting of the yards of people who would hire us was two or three dollars, and as soon as we got paid for a job, we took a break from employment by going to the drugstore. There we bought milk shakes, candy bars, and Pall Mall cigarettes, that brand because it provided smokes that were longer and stronger than most others. We repaired then to the closest empty lot, ate our candy, smoked our cigarettes, and talked about what we'd do when we were old enough to escape home and live on our own.

"You know one thing I will have," Winston once told me, puffing hard on his Pall Mall, and taking hits off a quart-sized Coke, "once I get grown?"

"What?" I said, drawing my own dose of smoke deep into my lungs and holding my cigarette the way James Dean did in *Rebel Without a Cause*, cool but necessary. "What's that, Winston?"

"I will have my damn cigarettes, that's what," he said. "As many as I want to."

"You're damn right," I said and flipped my butt into the street. "Let's see if that old lady on Hebert Street will let us cut her grass again. It's high as my knees."

What we really wanted was access to beer, but that was hard to come by. At age sixteen, I had already been introduced to the pleasures of alcohol by my cousin on my mother's side of the family, Addison Irwin in Maryland. I realized vaguely that I was to Addison Irwin, an older cousin from real people as opposed to the Duff bunch, as Winston was to me, but I didn't let myself think about that at the time. The comparison made me uncomfortable. If Addison considered my status and worth in the light I considered Winston's, I was on shaky ground. I didn't like the terms of the equation, and the way it figured socially.

I knew one thing clearly, though. I would never want Addison, my exalted cousin, to meet Winston, my lowly one, or to know I was related to someone like him. In the meantime, though, I liked cutting grass with Winston, eating sweets and smoking cigarettes with the money we made from our efforts, and having him look up to me as older, wiser, and more sophisticated. I wanted and needed the admiring approval he gave me, and I would take all of that he had to offer. He thought I was something, though I and the rest of the world knew different.

My family went back to East Texas later that summer, but in a few months my father did find a job on the Gulf Coast, working for the City of Nederland in the Streets and Alleys Department (which meant picking up garbage and digging ditches), and we had made that move out of the Piney Woods for good. By that time I was in my senior year of high school, and Winston was living with his family in a town named Fannett, twenty or so miles away.

I finished high school, enrolled as a commuter student at Lamar State College of Technology in Beaumont, and I had little reason to be around Winston, my young cousin living in the sticks.

But then Uncle Lewis moved his clan back to Nederland, Winston enrolled in the high school, which had been a power in Texas school-boy football for years, and he proved to be a defensive end of note. One of the coaches told me years later what made Winston so formidable at his position.

"When we played any team," he said, "they would run Winston's end sometime early on in the game. Let me tell you, hoss, once they ran it that one time, they didn't run it again for the rest of the game."

"He was that good?" I said.

"He was that mean," the coach said. "He wasn't that big, but nobody could stop him from getting to the ball carrier. He would do whatever it took to get there."

"And he took the ball carrier down."

"Winston Duff took it as a personal insult that somebody carrying a football would try to get around his end of the line. He made that running back pay his dues."

Winston got enough public notice in that football-crazed part of the world that people at Lamar began asking me if I was kin to him, and I allowed that I was. I even invited him to come to a retreat held by the fraternity to which I belonged, a collection of people too much on the fringe financially, ethnically, or intellectually to be members of any other social organization, even of the ones at Lamar. We had foreign students in the fraternity—Japanese and Arabs—and dolts and slackers, and others recognized to be misfits of many stripes and colors. We couldn't afford to be selective. But we did wear fraternity pins, and have meetings, and we did get drunk every chance we got.

Winston was a great hit at the fraternity retreat, held on someone's abandoned farm north of Beaumont in the palmettos and pines, and fueled with kegs of beer and random bottles of cheap liquor. At age sixteen, he drank with the best of them, not falling down and not throwing up, telling jokes and stories about playing football, and making his older cousin proud of him, a football end for the Nederland Bulldogs, destined to be recruited to play for a real university in the Southwest Conference someday.

That drunken weekend in and around the only building still standing on an abandoned and overgrown farm in Jefferson County, Texas, a tin-roofed barn full of drunken college boys, proved to be the height of Winston Duff's public regard and career, in my estimation, as I look back over the years.

Within a month's time, Winston's father moved his family north to Corrigan, a played-out sawmill town in rumpsprung Polk County in deep East Texas, and he took Winston with him. The head coach of the Nederland football team begged Lewis Duff to allow Winston to remain in the high school and on the team (which would have been illegal, but we're talking Nederland Bulldog football and we're talking keeping an advantage), living with him and his family in a subdivision tract house, in progress and on course to play out his eligibility and have a shot at attendance at a big-time Texas university where use might be found for him on the defensive end of some line in a large stadium in autumns to come.

My uncle would not allow that separation of his only son from the family, called on all the ties of kinship that bound his boy to him, and obliterated any chance for Joseph Winston Duff to escape the fate laid down for him by circumstance and blood. Winston listened to his father, accompanied the family to Corrigan, played football there in the obscurity of small-time East Texas, and dropped out of high school in his senior year, assuring that no ray of light would ever chance to fall upon him again.

The next time I saw Winston was at my mother's funeral at Menard Chapel in the 1960s. I was newly married, in graduate school in Arkansas, and Winston was working as a journeyman carpenter in the Beaumont area. He came up to me as soon as I arrived in the procession of cars escorting my mother's coffin into the woods of East Texas. He was wider in the shoulders than ever, rangy in the leg, and he was with a young pregnant blonde whose bra size looked to be larger than her IQ.

"Gerald," Winston said, grinning as we shook hands. "Aunt Dorothy was always so good to me when I was a kid and would come to y'all's house. This here is Jeanette. We're going to get married, I guess." And then to the blonde, "This here is my cousin Gerald, Jeanette. He's studying to be a college professor."

"Hidy," Jeanette said, staring over my shoulder at the woods behind me, proving that I was still not attractive to Texas women with big breasts. Talking to Winston, I was pained to see that his teeth had gotten bad, decay clearly visible on a couple of incisors, and more painful than that to me was that Winston was aware of the fact, holding his mouth funny and throwing a hand up to hide his teeth when he smiled or laughed.

"I bet you can't guess how much money I made last year," Winston said at one point, "building kitchen cabinets in new houses."

"How much?" I said, and then naming a figure I thought would be low enough to give him bragging rights when he answered the question he'd put to me, "six thousand?"

"I made over eleven thousand dollars," my cousin said. "And that was only what I had to declare to the government because of the paper they had on it. I really made a couple of more."

"Damn, Winston," I said, truly amazed at the amount of his earnings in that year in the '60s, "you're really making out all right."

He beamed, even forgetting to hide his teeth in his pride. During the funeral itself, Winston sat by me as I wept and mourned the death of my mother from cancer at age fifty-two, and I was glad to have my kinsman to lean on, literally and metaphorically, on that leafless, wet, and cold gray day in November on the burying ground of Menard Chapel. The coffin was cheap, and it was open for all to see my mother dead inside it. She had not wanted to be buried in those woods, as she called the Menard graveyard. The preacher for my mother's service was a cousin ordained as a Baptist minister, trying his best to justify what God had chosen in His infallible wisdom to do by subjecting Aunt Dorothy to such suffering and early death.

On that desperate ground, I wept and staggered about the graveyard physically supported by Cousin Winston as he tried to speak consoling words into my ear. He repeated my name over and over as though to convince me I was still myself, capable to survive that day and the others to come, unknown and perilous as they might be.

It was not until several years later that I heard of Winston again. I was living in Nashville, teaching at Vanderbilt, when my sister called me to bring me up to date on Duff family news. "Too bad about Winston," she said. "I guess you heard already."

"What? Is Winston dead?" I said, imagining a car wreck or an accident at work, something involving sudden violence and blood and finality.

"He might as well be," Nancy said. "He's about to go to the penitentiary in Huntsville. I don't know for how long, but it's got to be years."

"What did he do?" I asked, knowing Nancy would string out her telling of the tale for dramatic effect, true to the narrative sense of the Duffs, a clan relishing stories of disaster, loss, and abandonment. "Did he get caught robbing somebody?"

"No, Gerald," my sister said, exasperated at my leap to conclusion. "My goodness. Winston would never steal anything from anybody. He killed a couple of black guys outside some honky-tonk up in the Big Thicket, that's what."

"He shot them?"

"No, good lord. Winston wouldn't shoot anybody or stab them or anything like that. They got into some kind of argument or something inside the honky-tonk and when Winston went outside and got into his pickup to leave, these guys were waiting for him, I guess to beat him up, and Winston ran over them with the truck."

"And they put him in prison for murder? It wasn't called self defense?"

"I guess Winston could've got off with something like that, if that was all there was to it. But the thing is, see, after he knocked them down with the pickup, he backed up and ran over them again. That showed premeditation, the way the jury and judge saw it."

"Lord have mercy," I said. "And now he's in the pen. How stupid could he have been?"

"I expect he was drunk, too," Nancy said. "Not just stupid. So our cousin is a convict in the Huntsville pen. How do you like that?"

"I don't," I said. "I don't like it at all."

"I'm not going to visit him, either," Nancy said. "Are you?"

"How could I? I live in Tennessee."

"I'm just not going to think about it, my cousin in the pen," my sister said. "I've got enough on my mind as it is."

"Me too, Nancy," I said, "me too."

After that, I went back to Texas many times over the years for visits and anniversaries and graduations and deaths, but I never tried to see Winston in the state penitentiary in Huntsville, and I never asked any member of the family for any news about him. What news could there be? He had killed two men, been convicted and sentenced to confinement, and to think about him in that situation was something I would not allow myself to do. How would he look at me if I visited him in some special room for that in the prison? What would he say to me? What would he expect me to say back to him? What would he need from me that I was not prepared to give? Did he believe I had resources inside me that I could call on? I didn't think so. I didn't believe I did, no matter what my cousin might think.

I didn't want to have to try to summon up anything responsive to Winston's emotional need. I didn't want to discover what was inside me. Or what wasn't. I suspected I knew already how I would act, and I didn't want to admit that I could not and would not do my cousin any good in the worst time of his life.

After getting credit for good time served, Winston was released early from the Texas State Penitentiary in Huntsville on probation, and he returned to his work as a carpenter. I learned about his release indirectly, and I didn't try to find out where he was living and what he was doing. I did not want to contact him. I had told the woman who was my wife at the time about him, about my growing up with him, and what happened to put him in prison, and she made me swear not to let such a relative know anything about where we were living, where I worked, and who she was.

"Just what we need," she said. "A convict from Texas showing up in Gambier, Ohio, looking to reestablish old family ties."

I agreed with her, imagining Winston asking around Kenyon College in a search for his cousin. He'd be toothless, I figured, dressed in keeping with his social status, driving either a wreck of a car or a new pickup, and eager to see me. That reminder of my family and my origins I didn't need and could not have borne. I just won't think about him, I told myself. Winston couldn't find me anyway, and he'd never appear at my door, expecting me to respond to him as an older cousin from East Texas ought to do by reason of blood ties and memory.

I was right. Winston never wrote me, never called me, and never came to my door. I was never put to that test of blood. I did hear about him intermittently, though, again from my sister who had also risen socially and economically, in her case by marriage to a successful man in computers in Houston.

"Gerald," she said one night in a phone call, "guess what Winston did when he got back home to Buna?"

"Violated probation?" I said. "Ran over some more people? Stuck up a convenience store?"

"Don't joke. You know he's not like that. He wouldn't commit a crime. No, what he did was find out that that wife of his, Jeanette, had been messing around with Johnny Wooten while Winston was in the pen, and he beat the hell out of him. Broke the bones around one of Johnny's eye sockets. That's all he did."

"Johnny Wooten?" I said, "Betty's husband?"

Betty was one of Winston's sisters, and it was in her home with her husband Johnny that Winston had been directed to stay by the Texas State Department of Corrections while he served out his probation. His wife Jeanette had been living there with her two children by Winston while he was in Huntsville. I was not surprised to learn that Johnny had put a move on his brother-in-law's wife or that she had responded to him. The only thing out of the ordinary, I considered, was that Johnny had been stupid enough to think he could get away with it. He was not thinking at all, obviously. As my father would have said, Johnny wasn't thinking with his head.

"Did Johnny put the law on Winston?" I said. "Will the probation people send Winston back to the pen?"

"I don't expect Winston has anything to worry about from Johnny Wooten," my sister said. "Johnny knows what would happen to him if he breathed a word to anybody that could get Winston put back inside."

"Is Winston still staying at Betty's and Johnny's?" I said, knowing Nancy was right about Johnny Wooten taking his beating in silence. One would be enough.

"Winston has to until he gets permission to go off to live on his own, but that wife is gone now."

"Did Winston beat her up?"

"No," Nancy said in a disgusted tone. "You know Duffs don't hit women. They've not been raised like that."

"No," I agreed. "A Duff from East Texas will not physically whip up on a woman. He'll just wreak havoc on her mind."

Yet years later when I saw Winston for what was the final time, he was still living with his sister Betty and her husband Johnny Wooten, together somewhere in a small house in a dying town on the Texas Gulf Coast. As usual, that encounter with Winston took place at a funeral, the only event that ever draws all the extended Duff family together, this one the burial of my father in Menard Chapel with the rest of the clan and their connections by marriage and happenstance.

By then, I was even more of a curiosity to them than ever, though I had always been an oddity among the Duff bunch, as we were known in Polk County. All the clan remembered me as I was as a child. I was strange because I stuttered and talked at a hyperactive rate, I spent most of my time reading, impervious to calls for attention by other people, I was not athletic like most of my rangy, self-confident, supple cousins, people who shrugged off physical pain and emotional slights as they fought for possession of various kinds of balls, earning approval and admiration in the process. I was easily dissuaded, subject to fears and extended expressions of them, not prepared to be knocked down and get up again with blood in my mouth and in my mind with the intention to get payback for injury suffered.

My father's funeral was not nearly so riven with depression and foreboding for me as had been my mother's. When she died, she left a twelve-year-old daughter to be raised alone by my father, a man supremely unsuited for such a task. I was in my first year of graduate school, my first wife pregnant with our first child, no financial prospects in view, my older sister Nancy living in Seattle with her husband in a time when air flight to and from Texas, and paying for it, were comparable to sending a man to the moon. I was on the home ground alone.

Those years later at the funeral service for my father, dead at eighty-seven, things were different. It was high summer, and all the leaves were green. I was by then secure in my work. I was dean of a college in Memphis, I was the father of two accomplished and educated children, I was married to the woman right for me, I owned property, and I held title to university degrees and to professional respect. I had not been in my home country for longer than a day or two at a time in almost thirty years. I had worked myself free of the place I had come from, and I considered myself only technically a member of that Duff bunch in Polk County, Texas.

Yet when I saw Joseph Winston Duff standing in the shade of a sycamore at Menard Chapel on that hot day in August, I knew him instantly. And he knew me.

I was wearing a pin stripe suit and a dark tie, chosen from my closet by my wife because it was right for a funeral. She was not there, but back in our home in Memphis, because I didn't want her to see in one gathering in one place the clan of people I belonged to. She had expected to accompany me, since that was what her family members did in Alabama when someone died.

"You wouldn't like it," I told her. "You don't want to meet those people."

"What's to like or not like at a funeral?" she said. "Wives go with their husbands to the funerals of their husbands' parents. Don't they?"

"They do go all right. All of the family goes. That's the problem. If they all didn't go, I could take you with me. But every last one does go, and that's why I can't bear to have you there."

"Something's badly wrong," she said.

"Oh, yes. Badly wrong."

"With you and what you're saying, I mean," she had said.

Standing under the sycamore tree, old even when our great-grandfather preached at Menard Chapel, Winston looked at me with a quizzical tilt to his head, waiting to see if I would recognize him. He was wearing a blue jean jacket, a striped shirt, khaki pants, and his sleeked-back hair was showing signs of graying. Next to him were his sister Betty and her husband Johnny Wooten, the man who had seduced Winston's wife while he was in prison. All had been forgiven, or at least forgotten. The wife and children were long gone, but the Duff sister and brother were together.

"Winston," I said, and we embraced for the first time in our lives, such demonstrations of affection and relationship not having been cool all those years ago in the middle of the century. I greeted Betty and her husband, and Johnny reminded me of when he had fixed something gone wrong with my 1952 Dodge, a broken windshield wiper which had to function for me to be able to get a license plate. We laughed and joked, as people in East Texas do at funerals for those old enough to have had a long life. My mother had not reached that age, but my father had. The tone of the service was different, as a result, and my cousins felt free to josh and pick at me.

I remember two exchanges from that day, apart from my talk with Winston. Both were with Richardson brothers, the ones who'd knocked Pascal off his crutches all those years ago and paid for it, first cousins to me and older by several years. Both were basketball stars in high school and college, and both had careers as coaches of the sport.

Jesse Lee, the greater of the two in reputation and at one time coach of the basketball team in my high school, said to a group of relatives gathered around me in the graveyard, "Y'all might not know this, but Gerald tried to play basketball in high school."

"Naw," one of my aunts said, "Gerald was always a bookworm. He wasn't interested in ball."

"Yes, he was," Jesse Lee Richardson, once a Texas all-state center, said. "He was a bookworm, all right, but he wanted and tried to play basketball. Didn't you, Gerald?"

"I did," I admitted. "Jesse Lee's right, but I wasn't any good."

"He could not play a lick," my cousin said. "But look at him now. I expect he believes he's a self-made man, if anybody ever was."

A little later in the day, after the service was over and people had begun to drift away to drive back to town, the other brother, Wilson, asked me if I could hire him to coach basketball at Rhodes College. "I know how to manage inner city black players, Gerald," he said. "That's what y'all use in Memphis, and it takes special handling to get anything out of them."

I told Wilson to send his résumé to my office, though I didn't tell him I had nothing to do with hiring coaches and Rhodes College was an institution for upper-class white students who couldn't get into the likes of Vanderbilt and Duke, not a place for inner city blacks to run up and down the basketball court. He never did, and I knew he wouldn't, since getting a résumé together would have involved writing something down on paper.

Winston and I talked about the time I had taken him to the drunken Lamar fraternity retreat, about our summer cutting grass together to be able to buy cigarettes and ice cream, and finally he brought up the subject lurking behind all we were saying to each other.

"Gerald," he said, just after telling me that the most important thing my father, his Uncle Willie, had taught him was the use of Copenhagen snuff in the place of cigarettes, "I guess you heard about me and them black guys."

I couldn't look him in the eye after he had said that. Not because he actually hadn't called the men he had killed "black guys," but instead that epithet for blacks still the only label current in that place and with its people, but because I didn't want him to tell me about it. I did not want to know the details, I did not want to hear his story, I did not want his version of reality to be offered me. I did not want to hear the truth. Let all I knew about it just be what my sister had told me during our telephone conversations over the years. "Winston killed some black men. He ran over them with his truck. He's in the penitentiary. He's out now. He beat up Johnny Wooten for taking his wife to bed. He's living with Betty and Johnny now."

"I did hear that, Winston," I said. "I was sorry to hear about what happened."

Winston looked at my face, trying to get me to meet his gaze, and at that moment, our cousin Jewel, a retired school teacher, walked up to join what she thought was an ordinary conversation in the graveyard at Menard Chapel. It was not that. It was a confession, a remembrance, a reminder of blood, a plea for kinship, a claim. It was all that I did not want.

I jumped on the chance to accept the definition of the moment as Jewel imagined it to be, turning away from Winston's eyes and looking into hers.

"Jewel," I said. "Remember when you used to read to me when I was a kid? You would read whole novels to me and Nancy while we sat on the floor listening."

"I do remember," she said. "I can't believe now we all had the patience for that. Or the energy."

"It was a different time," I said, desperate to change the focus from what Winston had been wanting to say to me. "Kids wouldn't sit still for that now, would they?"

"No, they wouldn't," Jewel said. "What were y'all talking about when I walked up? Don't let me interrupt."

"Jewel," Winston said, his eyes still on me, "Gerald and I were just talking about the old days."

"The old days. What do you two boys know about the old days?"

"Lots. Gerald was real important to me back then when I was a kid."

"How was that?" Jewel said.

"Gerald taught me how to be bad," Winston said. "That's what he did for me. I looked up to him. He was my model. He led me to know how to be bad."

"Winston," Jewel said in a tone of dismissal and shock. "Surely not. You shouldn't say things like that. Don't make jokes. Gerald did not teach you how to be bad."

There in the graveyard at Menard Chapel, my father newly placed at rest in the earth for the long sleep that never ends, my kin all around the three of us, I knew in my bones and blood which one of the three cousins was telling the truth. It was not the retired schoolteacher. It was not the college dean. It was the convicted slaughterer of men, the boy who had pushed a lawn mower alongside me through the streets of Nederland, Texas, those years ago in the bright past, grown now into the only speaker of truth on that burying ground.

That recent dream about Winston and me from which I woke, that scene of him and me and a black man involved in a criminal act, had broken at the point where Winston was being led away in handcuffs. Just before he turned to enter the police car, he looked at me and made a gesture with his manacled hands, a sign of the kind you can interpret and believe only in dreams, since the waking world is never clearly seen and its message never certain. I knew what he was signaling. What he meant by the gesture in the dream was that he would take the blame. I was not to be afraid. I would not be found out. My cousin would be the sacrifice. In the dream I was grateful to my cousin, and I was determined to let him shoulder all burden of guilt. I would walk free, unsoiled and whole, and in the light of day. He would dwell in darkness and shame.

When I woke, I told myself that it was only a dream. It did not pertain to my life in this waking world, and it would slide away into obscurity, fade into nothing, as the days wear on. I will never see Winston again. I assured myself there in that dark room that I had never been complicit with him in any way. I was not guilty of theft. All I have I have earned by myself. I never taught him anything. He has nothing to do with me. It's all an accident of blood relationship. It will fade, it will vanish, it will go.

I need never think of him again, my cousin Joseph Winston, dead now and buried in some graveyard on the Gulf Coast, not at Menard Chapel. We were kin only in blood, not in kind. I tell myself that, but I know it's another one of my lies.

CHAPTER 33

From Honey Island to Menard Chapel

AT THIS POINT IN MY LIFE, HAVING JUST RETIRED FROM THE ACADEMIC WARS after ten years employment in an Illinois college, the truth of what Tolstoy once memorably said has powerfully kicked into my day-to-day existence. "Happy families are all alike; every unhappy family is unhappy in its own way," he said, and I've taken that to mean that nobody sees any reason to write about harmonious and gladsome situations. To describe my happy life with Pat, the successes my children have earned professionally and personally after finishing college and starting careers and their own families, and the placidity of my existence would bore me to do and any potential reader of such an account to suffer plowing through.

We want to read about pain, disaster, fear, dashed hope, regret, disappointment, bloodshed, betrayal, small-mindedness, and all other such flaws as flesh is heir to. Accomplishment, reward, success, compensation, pleasant maundering into peaceful old age—written account of all such even-keeled progress is naught but boredom and ennui.

The last novel I have published, though not the last one I've written, I called *Coasters*. I wrote that one in Baltimore, too, and I made use of the Texas Gulf Coast for setting and theme. Warren Murphy, my old partner in the electrical engineering lab during my pre-English major days at Lamar State College of Technology, I used as emblem of a man unable to break free from coasting and to achieve escape velocity from the Golden Triangle of Texas, try as he did to do so. Warren read the novel shortly before he succumbed to the wasting disease that took him, and he didn't recognize the protagonist as himself.

"I like the old boy, Gerald," Warren told me, "but he sure doesn't know how to handle his heavy dependence on poon tang, does he?"

"No, he doesn't, Warren," I told him. "But you got to give him credit. He's not about to give in and quit."

"No, he just keeps on sliding," Warren said. "Keeps on watching that big wheel turn."

Warren had achieved the advantage that distance provides. The making and the reading of fiction provides that relief and perspective, and I have always depended on the aid and kindness of imagined characters in settings as fully realized as I can make them to give me that distance I have yearned to find.

Menard Chapel is located in the far southeast corner of Polk County, just at the edge of the Big Thicket, an area now protected from development and change by the United States National Park Service. During the Civil War, deserters from the Confederate States of America and dodgers of the draft levied by that government lived deep in the Big Thicket on a bit of land elevated from the swamp. It was called Honey Island because of the supplies of that sugary substance found in the hollows of cypress and live oak and sweet gum growing there. These men who had fled a responsibility they would not accept swapped the honey they robbed from the hives to local residents for corn and meat and whiskey. It was a fair trade.

The Carter Lumber Company, quite able to cut all the virgin pine out of almost all that part of Texas, couldn't do anything profitable in the Big Thicket with teams of mules and horses and oxen, and later with trucks, because of the mud and water of the swamp, the presiding heat, the mosquitoes, and the general hellishness of the area.

Some of my earliest memories come from trips with my father and mother to Menard Chapel for funerals throughout the year, and each summer for the graveyard working. Relatives of the dead would come with hoes, shovels, axes, and rakes to clean the graves of weeds and brush, and with covered dishes of food for the picnic on the ground.

As I was growing up, I always thought my mother enjoyed going to Menard Chapel, at least for the graveyard-working, if not for the funerals. I remember her socializing with the Duffs and Murphys and Overstreets and Nowlens, and Richardsons, placing her contribution of food on one of the long tables, and listening to the gospel singing that always came after the cleaning of the graves and the eating of the picnic were at an end. My father, as Big Willie Duff, was in his element, telling stories and laughing and greeting everybody he hadn't seen since the last time he was at Menard. My mother followed him around, smiling and chatting, and keeping an eye on me and my sister as we tried to avoid the rowdiest of our cousins and the rough play of the other country children.

So when my mother was dying in Nederland in a small house on Seventh Street, and I came down from Fayetteville, Arkansas, where I was in graduate school, I was surprised at what she said to me that last time I saw her alive. The first subject she dealt with was my younger sister, Wilma, just twelve at the time.

"Gerald," she said, "promise me you'll take care of Wilma. She'll be here with Daddy, and you and Nancy won't be around. He won't know what to do."

"I will," I promised, and in due time, I did bring her to live with me in Illinois where she finished high school.

Then my mother looked at me, her blazing blue eyes huge because of the wasting effects of the cancer that was killing her, and said another thing.

"And Gerald, don't let them bury me there."

"At Menard Chapel?"

"Yes," she said. "Promise me you won't let them bury me in those woods. I'm not from there. Don't let them do that to me."

"I won't," I swore to her. "I won't let Daddy do that."

But when she died a couple of weeks later and I came to Nederland from Arkansas where I had gone when I abandoned her in her last few months of life, I let my father do just that.

"Where will Mama be buried?" I asked him.

"Why, Menard," he said. "Where all our people are buried. That's where she'll be."

I didn't fight him. I didn't know where else to have her buried. I had no money, and burial at Menard for a Duff cost nothing.

My last promise to my mother was a lie. She is buried there now, and until seventeen years after she had died, her grave was unmarked by a stone. Nancy and I put one up by hand ourselves in the summer of 1978 when I was at Rice University in Houston.

My father is buried beside her, and next to her grave is that of my sister Patricia Ann who died at birth, a year before I was born. Her grave is marked with a stone engraved with her name, the birth and death date the same day, and the words "Our Darling."

Each time I go to Texas I visit Menard Chapel, which is hard to find. You take the state highway south from Livingston, the road to Liberty, and turn onto a county road, half paved, and from that onto a dirt road to Menard Chapel. That road ends at the graveyard. There is no further you can go.

When I took my wife there the first time, she said nothing but to remark the beauty of the blue bonnets growing wild across the graves. The next time I took her she told me it was the most desolate and depressing place she had ever been. When I joked about our both being buried there someday, she said she would rise from the grave and walk back to Alabama if that took place. We laughed and looked about us at the abandoned chapel and the Texas state historical marker about my grandfather, and I knew she meant what she said.

I have spent my life lying about what I could not bear to accept as truth, and I have ended up writing fiction, lies about what happened to people I've imagined and who have never existed in this world. The lie has been my comfort and my refuge. Yet I know the truth when I see it. And I know that when I go in whatever form that leaving takes, I will remember my mother's eyes on me as I made her the promise I did not keep.

About the Author

In addition to writing fiction, poetry, and scholarly works, Gerald Duff has taught literature and writing at Vanderbilt University, Kenyon College, Rhodes College, and Johns Hopkins University. He has published eleven books, including *Indian Giver* and *Fire Ants*, which were finalists for both the Great Lakes Colleges Association First Novel Award and the Texas Institute of Letters Jesse Jones Award for the 2007 Best Book of Fiction. His other books of fiction and poetry have won the St. Andrews Prize for Poetry and the Cohen Award for Fiction, and have been nominated for the Edgar Allan Poe Award, the Texas Institute for Letters Award, the University of Michigan Literary Fiction Award, and the PEN/Faulkner Prize. *Home Truths* is his first book with TCU Press.